LOVE, LIGHT, *and* LAUGHTER

Monte Farber & Amy Zerner

Red Wheel
Boston, MA / York Beach, ME

First published in 2002 by
Red Wheel/Weiser, LLC
York Beach, ME
With offices at:
368 Congress Street
Boston, MA 02210
www.redwheelweiser.com

Library of Congress Cataloging-in-Publication Data

  Love, light & laughter : secrets of the enchanted couple / Monte Farber, Amy Zerner.
     p. cm.
  ISBN 1-59003-007-9 (alk. paper)
  1. Marriage—Miscellanea. 2. Farber, Monte—Marriage. 3. Zerner, Amy—Marriage. 4. Occultism. I. Title: Love, light, and laughter. II. Zerner, Amy. III. Title

  BF1439 .F36 2002
  646.7'8—dc21

                                                        2001048888

Typeset in 10 point ACaslon

Printed in the United States of America

MV

09 08 07 06 05 04 03 02
 8 7 6 5 4 3 2 1

The paper used in this publication meets the minimum requirements of the American National Standard for Information Sciences—Permanence of Paper for Printed Library Materials Z39.48-1992 (R1997).

We dedicate this book to our mothers, Jessie Spicer Zerner and Jennie Farber, and to our fathers, Ray Zerner and Lennie Farber, for giving us life, nurturing us to the best of their abilities, and showing us, by their successes and failures and how they dealt with them, how to live. Monte also wants to thank his aunt and uncle, Rosie and Morris Harth, and his stepmother, Doris Farber, for being there when he needed them most and, finally, his parents again, Jennie and Lennie, for not naming him and his sister Karen, Kenny and Penny.

We have created *Love, Light, and Laughter* to acquaint you with the art of love and to show you the steps you can take to bring love into your life. Whether you want to improve your existing relationship or meet your Soul Mate, *Love, Light, and Laughter* can light your way there and provide you with the means for getting in touch with the quiet voice within you that knows, without a doubt, what is best for your greatest good and highest joy.

Contents

Foreword

I suppose for people who need to put everything into categories, the use of concepts such as "Goddess," "Enchanted Couple," and the like, found on the pages following, will cause this to be labeled a "New Age" book. The sad thing about this label is that it creates the danger that only "New Age" people will gravitate to this book by Monte and Amy, thus causing it to miss its target audience: all human beings who have hearts.

Speaking personally, I don't have a New Age bone in my body. I'm strictly a "Father, Son, and Holy Spirit" man, myself. Have been, since my youth, and I'm now 74. Nonetheless, I loved this book and profited greatly from reading it, as I think you will too. Words, after all, are only the dress that thoughts wear. Beneath the temporal terms that these authors choose to use, lie eternal truths. Truths that they have discovered in their own life and experience.

And what a wonderful life and experience it is! I first met Monte and Amy on a cruise (of all places) and fell in love with them at first sight. What I loved about them was the way they were constantly, tenderly, together even in the midst of a crowd, yet always ready to move out from each other instantly, to help others around them. It was, and is, a relationship that makes you ache to see. In it are summed up the dreams so many have of what they would someday like to find in this life, on this earth.

Naturally if you've met them, you want to know instantly and at great length how they found this relationship of great price. They've written a book about it, you say? Get me that book! Yet *Love, Light, and Laughter* doesn't go down the paths you would expect. Instead of extolling the virtues of being together, it talks at length, from the outset, about the virtues of being alone. That's a surprise.

And there are many other surprises in this wonderful book! You cannot predict where it's going to go, or what the secrets of their relationship are. Just buy it, board the "enchanted world" express, and fasten your seat belts. You're in for a wonderful ride!

Richard N. Bolles, author of *What Color Is Your Parachute?*

Enchantment 'R' Us

When people first meet us, they frequently think that we're newly-weds, most likely on our second marriage. We find this puzzling, so we've asked why. People say it's because we seem to be having so much fun together and are so attentive to and respectful of each other. Now that's a sad commentary on the state of marriages today. Where is it written that long-term relationships can't be caring and exciting, full of love, light, and laughter? Certainly, not in this book!

It's true that we have absolutely no doubts about each other's love and commitment to our relationship, and that we thoroughly enjoy each other. In fact we are still as much in love (and in lust) as we were when we met back in 1974. We guess it shows.

For some years now, our friends and people who interview us have been calling us "The Enchanted Couple." It goes beyond the fact that we seem to have been blessed in the relationship department, although that is certainly true. We also work very hard at this thing called enchantment. We are the cocreators of nearly twenty self-help books and divination games and CD-ROMs, what we call our line of "spiritual power tools." *The Enchanted World of Amy Zerner and Monte Farber* has become our "brand."

We wrote *Love, Light, and Laughter* to share the story of how we made our relationship enchanted and how we have kept it that way. We're not thera-pists and we're not relationship gurus. But we do know the power of sharing stories. We hope and believe that our stories and relationship secrets, which you'll find throughout this book, will help you find an enchanted relationship and continue to build it over time. Sure, it requires effort to create an en-chanted relationship, but it's not nearly as hard as the alternatives—suffering

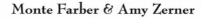

from loneliness or staying in a destructive relationship or one that prevents you from fulfilling your dreams and your destiny. Believe me: if we can find enchantment, you can, too.

Although we have created an extraordinary life for ourselves, and we make our living producing what many would call fantasy books and surrealist art, our definition of an enchanted marriage is quite matter-of-fact:

- Both partners put the relationship first, ahead of everything else.
- Both partners love each other for who each is, not just for who he or she would like the other to become.
- Both partners enjoy being dedicated to helping the other become more fully what each wants to be.

When we are in an enchanted state:

- We have harmonious relationships.
- Our faces are filled with love, light, and laughter.
- We know that we are loved.
- We are loving to children and animals.
- We take care of ourselves physically, mentally, and spiritually.
- Our sleep is deep and relaxed.
- We are well-liked in our communities.
- We have compassion and empathy toward others.
- We live peacefully.
- We enjoy the simple pleasures in life.
- We use our talents to bring happiness to others.
- We share our feelings.

We are aware of the danger of hubris in writing a book about our happy marriage. However, we can confidently say without fear of being struck down from on high that we are not going to be separated by discord or divorce. We wake up every morning knowing we are lucky to be alive and in love. We gratefully acknowledge our luck and whatever divine forces have helped us create our life together.

If it sounds like a fairy-tale existence—working together to create products of beauty and truth, living together happily ever after—in some ways it is. Fairy tales and other sacred myths help us understand our world and our place in it.

The absence of a myth illustrating how to live happily ever after has undoubtedly contributed to centuries of wildly romantic courtships, story-book weddings, and marriages from hell. This absence is a tragedy with ramifications well beyond the present.

However, the word *enchanted* itself offers a clue as to how we can actually go about attaining this exalted state. It is derived from the Latin *incantare* meaning "to sing into." We all know the powerful effect of inspiring music added to powerful words, which are then sung "into" us by a beautiful voice. We become enchanted, and no wonder! A great deal of thoughtful preparation and artistic skill has gone into making it happen.

A Life's Work

Sound the trumpets and let the truth be known throughout the enchanted realm! Living happily ever after is WORK. More accurately, a relationship, especially an enchanted marriage, is a work of art requiring consistent, thoughtful preparation, sensitivity and concern, ever-expanding awareness, and respect for one's partner. Everyone's—and we mean everyone's, including ours—relationships are threatened on a regular basis by a squad of dragons with names like Fear, Mistrust, Anger, Jealousy, Selfishness, Inflexibility, Low Self-Esteem, and those evil twin demons, Stupidity and Ignorance. These guys hang around at the gates of our enchanted castle banging to be let in. And believe us, once they get inside the door, they don't leave quietly. Pretending they're not there is worse than useless. They thrive when we try to ignore them. Blaming their existence on somebody else gives them a growth spurt. Dealing with them together, calmly and rationally, is really the only way to keep them outside ourselves and our relationships. And, like we said, that takes effort. We need to talk to each other, to show our love, to take care of ourselves, each other, and the relationship—every single day of our lives.

Until we started this book, we were too involved with our work and living our marriage to stop and think about exactly how we were doing it. When we began writing about it, we felt a bit like birds—so used to flying that we did not want to stop and think about how we do it for fear we'd get frightened and fall. However, we can take a hint, and the universe has been hinting about this book for a long time. Over the years, when we're lecturing to a large audience or meeting people casually, so many people have asked, "What's your secret for staying so happy for so long, living, working, and being together all the time?"

When our friends Michael Kerber and Jan Johnson, the President/CEO and Publisher, respectively, of Red Wheel/Weiser, asked us to write this book (that we have been calling our "art-o-biography") as a combination spiritual memoir and relationship book, we knew it was an idea whose time had come and we jumped at the chance.

We called the book *Love, Light, and Laughter* because we believe that these are the three most powerful forces available to us all in the creation of our relationships. They are the most valuable tools, in fact the only tools, that any of us has to surmount hate, darkness, and sorrow—the consequences of fear. "Love, light, and laughter" is also the closing salutation that we have been using for many years, in many letters, and in many books.

Love, Light, and Laughter is designed to take you on a guided journey, first to self-acceptance, and then to the creation of your own version of an enchanted relationship. We first offer you our unified take on the most important issues facing everyone interested in finding and maintaining a loving relationship. We then follow each issue with a personal story designed to entertain and enlighten as it reinforces the preceding message.

Part 1, "Finding Love," explores being alone and how it impacts finding one's Soul Mate. It goes on to offer guidance for finding love to those living alone, living with someone they like, living with someone they dislike, as well as how to find love if the issue of children is part of the mix. In this first section, the stories we share are about the good *and* the bad times of our relationship and what we learned from them all.

Part 2, "Lessons of Light," is a thorough examination of what it takes to keep a relationship thriving and moving forward. This is our special gift to you because it takes the book that is in your hands right now and turns it into your very own relationship oracle. Don't try to figure it out—that's our job. We are going to show you not one, not two, not three, but four different ways to use this oracle to access the information you need and incorporate it into your life on a daily basis.

Finally, part 3, "The Art of Laughter," is what we would call "a festive dance with the Muses" if we were advertising copywriters. Actually, there's no one in there but us crazy, enchanted people. In this third and final section, you will find some wild stories from both our private lives and from working together 24/7 to craft the business of *The Enchanted World of Amy Zerner and Monte Farber*, our "mom-and-pop entertainment conglomerate." We are not just talking about our creating the art and words for our extensive line of books, divination systems, and CD-ROMs, but agenting, manufacturing, promoting, and selling them on QVC and HSN, too! We are talking fine art, high fashion (Amy's *Spiritual Couture* is sold exclusively by Bergdorf Goodman in NYC), posters, music, candles, calendars, note cards, and jewelry that resulted in our seeing ourselves described in the *New York Times* as "The Martha Stewarts of the New Age." And every single story about all of the different aspects of our life comes back to the fact that we have worked so hard at so many things and succeeded (so far!) *because* we are each working with and for the person we love more than anyone else in this world or the next, our Soul Mate.

Love, now there's a subject—a cliché, a poem, a treatise, a theology, and much, much more. But what we mean by love is pretty simple. We mean saying, "I love you," and acting like it. We mean taking care of each other. We mean talking over problems. We mean clearing the air in a positive way. And we mean doing it every day.

Light—let it shine. Letting in the light means choosing the positive. It means being willing and able to see the best in ourselves and in each other. It means a whole chapter's worth of info.

Laughter will be obvious as you read some of the stories in this book. The old chestnut goes the unexamined life is not worth living. In our opinion, the life you can't laugh at isn't worth living. You'll see.

The Art of Love

Our goal has always been to make our life a work of art and our art a work of life. Staying together is an art, and all of us trying to bring love into our lives are artists. Every artist knows a creation of the moment *is* a creation of the moment, so fragile and delicate it can be ruined as easily as it can be strengthened. A most valuable lesson of being an artist is learning how to integrate the inevitable mistakes that are a part of developing—what we call the principle of the "controlled accident." Eventually, you learn to recognize, forgive, and even embrace these mistakes as opportunities to grow and create something original and wonderful.

Being full-time professional artists from well before the time we met may have indeed given us a head start. We have always been the kind of artists who integrate their personal growth with their art so as to expand awareness on the levels of body, mind, and spirit, both for us and for all who encounter our creations.

Of course we've had our trials and tribulations. Our original career efforts as fine artist and musician found us both face to face with an established art and music world controlled by people not nearly ready for spiritual music and art. Sometimes the pressures of dealing with our own bad habits, the rejections, and the confusion about which way to go next would wear us down and wash away our protective sense-of-humor coating. Then we would become dis-eased and say and do things we would come to regret. We are going to tell you those stories, too. Our genuine affection for each other and the insights born of our metaphysical studies have always kept our hearts from hardening toward each other in times of sorrow or during the inevitable mistakes of growing.

Our marriage has thrived even under the tremendous pressures involved with producing and marketing—what we like to think of as nurturing—our nearly twenty books and products, our "children," as we are fond of calling them. Our works are divination systems, in the sense that they enable us all to contact the divine within us. We usually call them *spiritual power tools* because they are designed to help us all build our spiritual lives—which we define as our divine mechanism for creating our own reality—the way power tools help builders to build things faster and more easily. We have come to see our family of oracles as sacred adult children's books allowing us to contact and satisfy the yearning of the child within for meaningful play and its consequent empowerment. This realization coincided with Amy being asked to create a series of three unique children's books with her late and much-missed mother, Jessie Spicer Zerner, entitled *Zen ABC*, *Scheherazade's Cat*, and *The Dream Quilt*.

It's a situation very much like our marriage: our creations are fun, practical, and very successful but they are hard to categorize. Being original and ahead of our time, like every other aspect of life on this plane of duality, has its strengths and weaknesses. We learn a lot from what we do every day. We're proud of it and our hearts are usually filled with joy because we are succeeding against heavy odds in getting our art out to a world that so obviously needs it. But we're also sad or discouraged sometimes when we put our souls on the line with our art only to find we are misunderstood, undervalued, or rejected by the marketplace.

We will never forget when a powerful corporate art buyer spent an hour gushing over a dozen of Amy's incredible fabric collage tapestries, going on and on about how they were the most beautiful, complex, breathtaking, high art she had ever seen by a woman or a man, only to put down her glasses, look Amy in the eye, and say without a trace of embarrassment or irony at what she said, "Can you make some tapestries that are not so incredibly beautiful? People in the offices and boardrooms I decorate wouldn't be able to concentrate on their business!"

We tried to get her to see that being inspired by art that transports you to the highest realms of your being would help all of these business people be more creative and intuitive, but she was not about to take the chance that we were wrong. We hope that you will take the chance that we are right and let us share with you what we have learned about creating love.

It's a good thing that all of our artistic creations, including our enchanted relationship, do indeed have the power to heal, inspire, and energize because we need that, too, every day. Doesn't everybody? And even if you don't make art or work as a healer, you still have the power to heal yourself and your relationships, to live fully and creatively. We have tried to write *Love, Light, and Laughter* to not only reveal how we've done it, but also to help you discover your own creative, self-healing, and true love-producing abilities.

> **Secret: Visualize your wishes in your mind's eye.** Become aware of the tone and subject matter of your moment-to-moment inner dialogue. Visualize what it is you want with all your heart. See it with your inner sight and feel it as if you were really there, experiencing it with all of your senses. Practice visualization every day. Our dreams help us to create our material reality as surely as our material reality helps us to create our dreams.

Through our art, we seek to contact, portray, and make practical use of the numerous unseen forces that surround and sustain us. Amy's resplendent tapestries are a visual representation of those unseen forces. Our work revives the ancient tradition of using art, sacred objects, and ritual to both remind and enable everyone to tap in to these energizing and rejuvenating energies.

It feels satisfying to know beyond a doubt that you can fulfill your life's highest purpose. That knowledge is also useful in your effort to create your enchanted marriage, especially helpful during those times when those inevitable growing pains tug at you and your partner's resolve. Like the birds we likened ourselves to earlier, we know it's not how far you fall but how soon you catch yourself and start flying again that counts.

PART I

Finding Love

CHAPTER ONE

Finding Love
if You Are Alone

(Hint: We All Are Alone So Read This Chapter!)

S ome people enjoy living with one person or more. Yet it is obvious that some people like to live alone, even some of the ones who say they desperately want someone to share their life with.

In the free world, we're privileged with the choice to explore all available aspects of life, if and when we so desire. We can choose to accept the conventional wisdom about our possibilities, given the circumstances of our birth and beyond, or we can choose to blaze a new trail and create new definitions of what is possible.

The meaning of your life is to give your life meaning. In our search to find our special gifts and to use them, everyone has to go through different phases in life that may alternate between desires to be either social or solitary. We believe that everyone should live alone for a time. Living alone may prove to be the best way for you to bring love, light, and laughter into your life and the lives you touch.

It is a pity when someone does not realize that living alone is just as valid a choice for a life of quality and meaning as a life lived with a Soul Mate in the next room. We feel extremely fortunate, blessed in fact, to have found each other, and we have worked harder than most people to make our good fortune last, but that does not comment on or diminish anyone else's life choice.

Whether or not you decide to live alone or with another, problems will arise when people fail to be true to themselves and instead perform according to others' expectations. It is important not to be afraid to admit to others or to yourself that you really do like living alone and do not want anyone disturbing your hard-won sovereignty over yourself.

How Do You Feel About Being Alone?

Inscribed upon the two pillars at the entrance to the Oracle at Delphi were the two essential pieces of advice for having a successful and healthy life: "Nothing in excess," and "Know thyself."

We all are alone, every one of us, and in many ways. At times the two of us feel alone because there do not seem to be many couples who have our kind of relationship. Inventing your own artistic style or trying to brush the "dirt" of ignorance and superstition off the buried treasure chest of ancient wisdom to be found in what has been mistakenly called the "occult" is a real challenge! As the saying goes, you can always tell the pioneers; they're the ones with the arrows in their backs.

Being true to yourself, expressing your creative self fully, and finding your Soul Mate will not guarantee a life free of suffering. It does mean that you will have a partner to share your burdens and that your life will be much more enjoyable and meaningful.

Secret: Growth comes through self-examination and self-awareness. Know thyself. In our case, it was our commitment to our mutual goal of personal and artistic development that has allowed us to learn and help each other grow. We may not know the meaning of life, but we have come to know the meaning of our life.

According to the Prussian Colonel von Klauswitz, the great military strategist, the first rule of warfare is, "Make your base secure." This rule works just as well for anyone with a goal. Our first and greatest "enemy," or obstacle, is usually our own self, or, more accurately, that self's fears. (Von Klauswitz is probably more known for another quote, "Love is war through other means," but thankfully, that does not apply in our enchanted world.)

A hero is just as afraid as a coward, but goes on in spite of her fears. All of us have these same fears, and the successful among us are the ones who go on anyway. By using plans and rules and the advice of elders and wise people as our armor and our army, we can all win our personal battle for love, contentment, and material success.

You cannot move on to finding your Soul Mate if you are unduly uncomfortable with being alone. You build a house by starting with a strong foundation, the same way you write books and build strong relationships. People secure enough to live alone can find the confidence in themselves to take risks in both relationships and on big projects.

The foundation of a committed relationship is the two people in it. If anyone in a relationship feels very insecure about himself or herself for whatever reason, real or imagined, the relationship itself will feel insecure, and it will eventually prove unsatisfying. If one or both of those people secretly yearns to live alone, or if the temperaments involved are unsuitable for cohabitation and no one wants to admit it, all the books in the world won't help them to find true love. True love is true acceptance: acceptance of self and of the beloved.

How do you feel about being alone? This is not a trick question. There is an old saying, "For every pot, there is a lid," a clever way of suggesting that there is a perfect match for everyone. However, people are not pots and choosing to live by yourself is a valid life choice. If you are living alone now, it is important for you to honestly appraise your feelings about your situation without being unduly influenced by the endless pressures from your family, friends, and our entire culture to partner up, marry up, and hurry up, and have children. If you learn nothing else from our book, please learn that you have the right to decide the kind of life you want to experience, no matter what anyone else says.

It is more than okay if you like to be alone. If people have a hard time being alone, there is a good chance that they don't like themselves or their present situation and don't want any reflection time. Those who do not like to be alone may be trying to distract themselves from past pains, from having to make hard choices in the present moment, or from some aspect of the past, present, or future that frightens them. There are some people who believe that they can only figure out who they are and what they want by having other people around to tell them or to judge them. Once again, these are all valid life choices, as long as they are consciously chosen.

Whether you are alone or in a relationship, it is critically important that you do not look outside of yourself for someone to help you feel fulfilled and complete. You can only feel fulfilled and complete if you make an effort to understand yourself and to accept yourself as you are. We are all growing. Being committed to growing lovingly and consciously makes life a magical adventure. We must never stop loving ourselves and lose sight of the fact that most of us are fine just the way we are. Our real problem is believing that we are not.

AMY: PORTRAIT OF A VERY YOUNG ARTIST

I loved living in Laporte, a town of 175 people that was the county seat of Sullivan County, part of the gorgeous Endless Mountains area of Pennsylvania. It was a safe, idyllic place to grow up. I have never had a problem being alone because making art is a solitary pursuit, and I have always been an artist.

My first memory is sitting on the knee of my maternal grandfather, Clayton Spicer, painting leaves on the trees of one of his paintings. "Claytie," as we called him, was a masterful painter who had studied at the Art Students League in New York City with Robert Henri, author of *The Art Spirit* and the founder of the Ashcan School of American art. It was there that he met my grandmother, Lilias, a fellow student whose natural artistic ability matured into a flare for interior design work for W. J. Sloans, an important New York City department store of the time.

My mother, Jessie Spicer Zerner, told me that she never had to worry about me being a bored or lonely child because I was quite content to be alone and, though she was always coming up with projects for us to do together, I was also happy to sit by myself and draw, color, paint, do crafts, and make what we called "dish gardens." I would get a big dish and go on one of my frequent trips through the woods alone and get different mosses and mushrooms and a plant called Jack-in-the-pulpit. My favorite part was getting the mirror to look like a little pool. I feel they were forerunners of my collaged landscapes.

MONTE: BEING DIFFERENT

Until I met Amy, I always felt very alone, even in a crowded room. Today, I am perfectly comfortable being alone and with being an original thinker, inventor, and philosopher, but this was not always the case. I have always been—well, different. From my early childhood, it was painful to me to realize that I was so very different from my friends and other people, especially my parents.

My parents struggled to overcome their childhood traumas, their efforts worsened by the shame-based secrecy they maintained. It prevented them from obtaining loving support from each other or anyone else. Their problems were brought to the boiling point by having children, first me, and then my sister, Karen, a couple of years later. Though they did the best they could under very difficult circumstances, they were so distracted by their struggle to survive mentally, physically, and emotionally that there was not much room in their consciousness for the kind of unconditional love, focused attention, and secure nurturing that children need.

I have come to love both my parents, but until I was a teenager, I not only felt emotionally isolated but was physically abandoned by my mother's frequent long hospitalizations for depression and my father's grueling schedule as a rookie New York City policeman—a never-ending cycle of 8:00 A.M. to 4:00 P.M. one week, 4:00 until midnight the next week after forty-eight hours off, and then midnight to 8:00 A.M. the next week. When I try to remember him during my childhood, all I see is a sleeping form sprawled across their troubled marriage bed. They divorced when I was twelve.

Were it not for the caring and self-sacrifice of my aunt Rosie, who lived across the street from us and came over frequently to help, and my uncle Morris, who straightened me out about a lot of things when I visited him in swinging old England for that most exciting summer of 1964 (the "Triple Crown" of the Beatles, Carnaby Street, and Shakespeare's 400th birthday celebration!), I believe that my early life would have crushed a lot of the sweetness out of me and made it much harder for me to bring love into my life.

Everyone Needs to Be Alone Sometimes

Even Soul Mates need to be alone sometimes. Everyone needs to have a place in the world that allows him to process the events of his life, to get in touch with how he feels mentally, physically, emotionally, and spiritually, and to plan for the future. Being alone in your sacred space can produce many of the benefits of meditation: clarity of thought, calmness, and a higher, more generous perspective when you emerge.

By far, the most important function served by a sacred space is the sense it can offer of being connected to and supported by the forces of peace, beauty, and your personal concept of the Divine. The purpose of this book is to help you make your relationship a sacred space, too. The sacred should not be reserved just for "holy" places and houses of worship. Having a quiet place in nature where you can be alone and undisturbed is the ideal as far as we are concerned.

> **Secret: Nature teaches us about the cycles of life.** The entire world is alive with messages and it speaks to us, if we will only listen. Nature reminds us of the abundant beauty present in everyday life. Make a time and space in your day when and where you won't be disturbed, so you can listen to all that is good in your life "speak." The goal is to be so in harmony with your life's purpose that you will instinctively know which paths to follow from the many that present themselves each day.

Secure your home and your relationship as your base. Respect it by making it beautiful and nourishing to your senses and your spirit. To neglect your

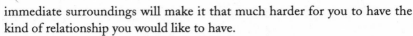

immediate surroundings will make it that much harder for you to have the kind of relationship you would like to have.

It is crucial to your development for you to have a place where you can lock the door when you want to and feel untouchable. It can be anything from a converted closet, like the one I had in my bachelor pad, to a house-sized studio such as we built for Amy. The important thing is that it be a place where you know you are safe, secure, and in touch with your essence, spirit guides, and any and all things you hold dear. It is a good idea to create a personal altar in your sacred space upon which to place reminders of your goals and what you hold sacred. There are so many pressures and distractions every day that we cannot have too many reminders of what is important in our lives.

If you live alone, you know the luxury of coming home after a busy, noisy day to the peace and quiet of a home that is just the way you left it. You do not have to answer to anyone, either literally or figuratively. Literally, because you can let your answering machine take your calls, and figuratively, because you do not have to explain your actions or your inaction to anyone. If you are alone now but seeking to bring your Soul Mate into your life, be grateful that you have a place where you can be undisturbed when you need to recharge your spiritual power supply.

It is so important that it bears repeating that you must have your own sacred space if you live with your committed partner, any children, your parents or other relatives, your friends, roommates, or even fellow soldiers in a barracks. You need at least one place that can be yours and yours alone, even if only for a little while.

If the circumstances of your life have prevented your access to this important requirement for peace of mind, please find one immediately! Not having a place to call your own makes it much harder for even the most disciplined people to accomplish their goals.

MONTE: OUT ON MY OWN

When I was seventeen, my father threw me out of the Brooklyn apartment I had grown up in, right next to beautiful Prospect Park. We had been sharing it for a couple of years, just the two of us, and I thought things were going great. However, our bond suffered as my presence in the house became more and more like bondage for "Bubsie," the nickname my father earned from his fellow NYPD cops for his devil-may-care, Lothario personality. Fathering a teenage son is hard enough, but living with one when the father was single, making up for lost time after a horrible marriage and, most importantly, hadn't stopped being a teenager himself turned out to be catastrophic.

The reason I was thrown out of my house was that I didn't come visit my father in the hospital when he was admitted after fainting in a subway car. The doctors discovered that my father was suffering from tachycardia arrhythmia, an irregular heartbeat, which I believe was brought on by all the stress of his life that he never let show.

When he called from his sickbed to tell me where he was, he had made a point of saying, "Don't come visit me. This place is in a bad neighborhood and I'll be home on Tuesday." So, obedient and hospital-shy child that I was, I didn't visit.

When Tuesday rolled around and he didn't come home, I called to find out where he was. It was as if it was his turn to start doing time in a mental hospital. "Why didn't you come see me?" he roared into the phone. "They thought I was going to die! They took my shield and my gun! I want you out of there before I come home." And then he hung up. In a daze, I took what I could carry and became homeless. For a while I really called Prospect Park my home, sleeping on benches I had played on as a child.

Getting thrown out of my house at seventeen years old for such a stupid reason was so embarrassing that I lied to my pseudo-hippy friends that my father had done it because he had found lots of drugs in my room. They knew I was lying because, though I was a budding musician, I had very pointedly and very loudly never done drugs before and had, in fact, threatened in all seriousness to kill any of them who followed through on their threat to get me high by surreptitiously slipping LSD into my soda, which they never did, I'm glad to say.

After I got really tired of living in the park—it was summer—I was taken in for a few weeks by my friend, a great guitarist who was eating macrobiotically so he could get higher when he injected heroin into his pure veins. As anyone who lived through the sixties can tell you, this kind of health regimen was no crazier than those times. His Jamaican roommate, apparently a drug dealer, was murdered in the house a week after I moved out. It was a message lost on the both of us. I began to smoke marijuana and did so for quite some time. My lack of a place in my life to call my own wreaked havoc with every aspect of my life and my decision-making ability.

My homeless period was a long, arduous rite of passage into manhood. At first, I was devastated and frightened to the point of a strange numbness. As I was forced to depend totally on myself for everything, I learned how to go to the sacred space within myself for advice and solace and the power to go on, no matter what life dealt me. I have also learned that the wonderful conditions of my daily life are an outward manifestation of the rich inner life I continue to consciously cocreate every day.

The power of love works miracles, and one of them is that I put those crazy times behind me. Eventually, thanks to my own efforts and the loving support of Amy and her mother, Jessie, I learned who I was and who I was meant to be. Having the secure, sacred space of both our home and our relationship revealed the many ways my youth was still affecting me, such as my tendency to get very nervous and, according to Amy, irritated when things don't make sense to me or when I think people are acting crazy. I suppose it feels too much like my childhood.

AMY: MY SACRED SPACE

In the ancient world, it was an accepted custom that when a person reached a certain level of development, either intellectual, spiritual, or financial, she would build a temple to proclaim and share her good fortune with her contemporaries and with the divine forces from whom all blessings flow. Though our entire home is constantly evolving toward becoming a sort of spiritual center, my large, two-story, mauve-colored studio has served as the sacred birthing place for my work and the center for all of our other activities, too.

In 1987, Monte was working on perfecting his *Karma Cards* for Eddison/Sadd Editions, the British book packager who had sold the project to Penguin Books. I had just been awarded a fifteen-thousand-dollar United States National Endowment for the Arts Fellowship grant in the category of Painting, not Crafts, for my fabric collage tapestries, which I consider "paintings" because I conceive of my work exactly as a painter does. I think of myself as an artist, not as a fabric artist. The fabrics, ribbons, laces, appliqués, trimmings, and thousands of other objects that fill the bins and shelves of the second floor of my studio are my "paint." Even though all of my work is sewn together, and I'm the only artist in the history of the NEA to win an award in the Painting category for work made entirely of fabric, I hate to sew. I will not even sew a button onto our clothes, because I spend so much time sewing for my work.

Our astrologer and friend, Leor Warner, wisely advised me to apply for an NEA grant and to do so in the Painting category. Having taken his advice and been fortunate enough to win a major grant on my first application, I began working hard on my fellowship project, a series of five very large tapestries, nine feet long by six feet high, depicting the five elements of traditional Western metaphysical thought, Fire, Air, Water, Earth, and Ether, or pure energy.

I make my tapestries on the floor. Since 1975, I had made over a hundred tapestry collages in a room barely big enough for me to walk around even one of them. We decided to take a leap of faith on behalf of ourselves and our careers. We arranged with my sweet mother, in whose house we were living, to both buy my house from her and to refinance it so that we could build a large studio for me and my materials. "Ma," as everyone called her, was happy with this solution. It enabled her to travel more and have us fix up the house the three of us called home.

In the winter of 1987, I supervised Monte's design and then the construction of my large, two-story studio, which we consecrated as a temple using ancient techniques. Monte marched around the cinderblock foundation seven times forward and seven times backward, nearly falling into the hole at least seven times. We wrote our favorite sayings on the walls with heavy felt markers, like metaphysical graffiti artists, and though the carpenters thought us a bit strange, I think they liked it. Before the large wooden beams for the floor arrived, we put crystals and jewels in the holes of the cinderblocks, each placement accompanied by a different temple blessing prayer from a different culture. We wanted my studio to be a consecrated temple to The Goddess.

The only regret that we had about clearing the scrub oak and brush from the studio site was that one large oak tree had to be cut down. We had both prayed and asked that the spirit of the tree come live in my studio, and I am convinced our invitation was accepted. We heard a commotion among the carpenters the day the big foundation beams arrived. They knew what we had done and told us in reverential voices that they had never seen wood this clear of knots in such large beams. We knew then that I would soon be moving into a truly sacred space.

Traditionally, the temple provides the ritual space for moving up along the *axis mundi*, what the ancients called the cosmic axis. The axis mundi provides a center to the cosmos by connecting the underworld to our realm and to the heavens. It may take form as bridge or ladder shapes, which I often see emerging in my work. The ladder shapes or other axis mundi manifestations lead us from the mundane into the spiritual world. The ascent along the axis mundi also represents transcendence over illusion.

Monte and I are constantly working on numerous business projects, so our house sometimes seems like a factory with bedrooms. Although we have chosen to be together and work together as much as we can, we have evolved our individual schedules in shifts, like those in a firehouse: someone is always on duty. I get up and go to bed early, taking care of all of the things that have to be done in the mornings including talking to early risers and our European

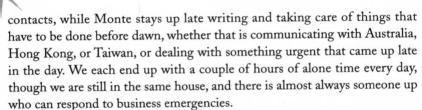

contacts, while Monte stays up late writing and taking care of things that have to be done before dawn, whether that is communicating with Australia, Hong Kong, or Taiwan, or dealing with something urgent that came up late in the day. We each end up with a couple of hours of alone time every day, though we are still in the same house, and there is almost always someone up who can respond to business emergencies.

Though the daily grind of business is often difficult, I take great pleasure in combining all the individual images, colors, symbols, and layers of my tapestries and in making each one of them a sacred space. My artwork allows me to live every day feeling that I am in direct communication with the transcendent realms. This is an immensely powerful and important thing to do.

To commune with the wisdom of the sacred realms is as essential to us as eating, drinking, breathing, and dreaming—if we are to function fully in the world. My art and my studio are tangible examples of the powerful beauty possible on Earth by the wisdom of making a relationship a sacred space. This ancient but always fresh concept beckons us to the sacred sanctuary found in every loving heart.

> **Secret: Peace begins when expectations end.** There is goodness in things as they are—accept the greater purpose behind frustrating circumstances. The present moment is your point of power. The secret of contentment can't be gained from achievements in the world but only from finding your inner peace.

Are You a Tiger or a Swan?

We laugh when we hear people referring to "unreasonable expectations" because we know that *all* expectations are unreasonable; no one is guaranteed another breath, let alone winning the lottery. Such is the case when people ask, "How can you stand being together all the time?" But they might just as well be asking someone else, "How can you stand to live alone?" Unless we are able to imagine someone else's situation from his point of view, we will not only misjudge him, we will miss out on new ways of thinking and living that we might love.

> **Secret: Judgment has its time and place.** Let it help you be relentless in your pursuit of truth and the deeper implications of whatever situation you are in. Remember, criticism must be constructive, not a smokescreen for hurtful words and deeds. Judge the truth and judge the lies.

There are as many reasons to live alone as there are people who do so. Our studies of ancient wisdom teachings and our personal experience have taught us without a doubt that everyone is at the place in her life where her past actions, strong beliefs, and fervent desires have brought her. The present moment is just that: a present, a gift. In the present moment you have a most precious gift: the power to change your future. You can do so by consciously directing and controlling your actions; examining, questioning, and adjusting your beliefs; and bringing your desires in line with your goals.

If your past has brought you to a lonely place, find out why and change your life and self so that you *can* feel comfortable being alone. It will not happen overnight, but it will happen if you decide that you want it to happen. Simply denying you feel that way, or saying "I don't like being alone," and then bringing someone into your life and, worse, into your home, without addressing the underlying problems will jeopardize even the most promising relationship.

Some people, like the writer Henry David Thoreau, wish to hear the quiet voice within themselves and within nature, a voice only audible in solitude. Some people become nuns or monks, attached to a religious organization, or go alone as hermits. Most people who are shy or need a lot of privacy choose less total forms of withdrawal. They are usually self-aware enough to realize that they don't want the distractions of cohabitation, period. In the past, social critics have unkindly deemed such people "confirmed bachelors," "spinsters," or "loners."

The desire to name and label everything is a natural one. But it is time to honor the fact that we are all, every one of us, alone and in many different ways, too. To do so, we propose a new term to describe those whose extraordinary need to be alone is a glorious reminder to us all of our basic alone-ness. These people have friends and lovers. They love just as much as we do, maybe more, for every wisdom tradition teaches that sitting in silence produces great wisdom, compassion, and love. From now on, let us agree to call these people "Tigers," because their version of love is more like that of the incredibly powerful, beautiful, and endangered tigers of Asia that live alone in the jungle and only associate with other tigers when they want to mate.

We are of the "Swan" persuasion. Swans mate for life and spend most of their time with each other. Though we are mated for life and hope to be together beyond this world as well, a person does not have to have a romantic relationship with a person to be a member of the Swan tribe. If you are looking for a soul connection and a life with your Soul Mate when you finally discover each other, you are a Swan.

Just remember that, although Swans and Soul Mates can be fiercely protective of each other, they almost never turn their fierceness on each other and, if they do, they immediately recognize their mistake, ask forgiveness, and kiss and make up. The unfortunate phenomena of the "macho" male distorts a man's true role, which is to serve and protect his Soul Mate and family.

Great love transcends time, the physical world, and all categories. We have met lots of people who are obviously Soul Mates but who are not in a romantic relationship. Still they have incredibly close, spiritual, and sometimes psychic connections. They can be best friends, siblings, relatives, or parent and child.

AMY: MY MOTHER

Although she is no longer with me in the flesh, I will love my mother forever. Telling you about her is more relevant to my development as a person and an artist than if I filled this whole book with the individual events of my life. I was a mama's girl. I lived with my mother for almost forty-six years, and Monte and I miss her terribly. We all lived together in the same house, which was unusual. She was our mother, our best friend, our artistic collaborator, and occasionally our only child.

Without Ma, there would be no "Enchanted World of Amy Zerner and Monte Farber," and not just because I would not have been born. She helped us in more ways than I can say. She showed me how to be a working artist, and I am proud to follow in her footsteps. Her love for life and for her family and her dedication to her work inspired everyone who knew her. We were always close but became even closer when my father, Raymond, died of a heart attack while driving to pick me up from graduation practice at East Hampton High School in 1969. Though she was devastated and felt like joining him on the other side, she stayed for me, my sister, Toni, and my brother, Peter.

I learned from Ma's gentle guidance that the key to being a successful artist was simple: if you are not failing, you are not trying. She even managed to tell me this in such a way that I was never aware that my work was anything less than wonderful. I remember being four years old and making my first garment for my mother for Mother's Day. Even though I knew it was lopsided, my mother oooohed and ahhhhhed over what I had done.

But she was a great critic and would not give praise undeservedly. When she crossed over, I wondered how I could ever make another piece without her seeing it and giving me hints and advice, but she assured me on her dying day that she would always be there if I needed her. She knew how much I depended on her guidance. I do feel her now, always with a helpful, loving hand and her wonderful laugh.

We were not together every day. Monte and I traveled frequently, doing lectures, workshops, and our annual Inner Voyage cruises. My mother had a boyfriend in Vienna, where she maintained an apartment year round and visited for two months twice a year. Unfortunately, she was in Vienna on April 26th, 1986, and for weeks afterward, when the Chernobyl nuclear reactor in Ukraine suffered a major accident and released poisonous quantities of radioactive gases and dust into the air. Ten years later, she was dead from severe leukemia, brought on by myelofibrosis, a rare radiation-caused disease found frequently in Europe after Chernobyl.

When Ma got sick, she told us that she did notice and clean up a lot of dust on the patio of her Vienna apartment for a couple of days before the cowardly Soviet Union finally told the world what had happened. Losing someone we loved totally reinforced our already strong dislike for nuclear-generated power, something we had worked against here on Long Island for many years.

In 1985, Monte was working as the location manager of the movie *The Money Pit* and asked his boss if he could go home early that Friday night because his mother-in-law was coming back home from Vienna after two months, and he had really missed her. His boss looked at him incredulously and told him that he was really scraping the bottom of the excuses barrel. It took Monte twenty minutes to convince him that he was serious and, after his boss heard that we all lived together, another ten to convince him that he, Monte, was not "St. Pussywhipped," the patron saint of mothers-in-law!

My mother and I talked about everything. She had let me pick out whatever clothes I wanted when I was a kid and encouraged me to be an individual when I was a teenager. She contributed greatly to all of our work and to our enchanted marriage, too. Even now, it is difficult for us to return home from one of our merry adventures, our Inner Voyage cruises, a Hamptons or New York City party, a book tour, a convention, or any trip and not have her there to hear our stories. Her caring and insight really complemented and completed everything.

I can easily see her hunched over her drawing table at all hours of the day and night, working feverishly because she loved her work, which was usually drawing animals, children, and illustrating fairy tales, which let her live in a sweeter and gentler world. I suppose that is another thing that I have inherited from her. She was a master at pen-and-ink drawing, and her impeccable sense of color, style, and design was a gift that she inherited from both sides of her family.

Though she was an artistic prodigy who graduated from Pratt Institute in only one year, she was a truly spiritual person who never flaunted her brilliance and made everyone she met feel better. She devoted herself to the small things that make life worth living. Everyone who spoke at her memorial, as well as the hundred people who came to my studio where it was held, all commented on how remarkable she was. A friend of hers, a Jewish cantor who was also a printer and had worked with her on several books, called her a "Zedek," a truly rare and righteous person. He told me with a smile that to call someone a righteous person, especially a "shiksa" (non-Jew) like my mother, was the highest compliment he was capable of giving.

Ma also inspired generations of children through the dozens of coloring and activity books she designed for Waldman Publishing. During the twenty-five years she worked for them, she befriended Israel Waldman, the company's founder. She not only supplied him and everyone she came in contact there with art, but with her wise counsel, and she helped many of them get through some horrific times.

The day after she died, we called Mr. Waldman's home to break the news to him, only to find out that we had interrupted the memorial ceremony going on at his home. He had died of a heart attack the same day as my mother and within minutes of her passing! I knew he'd always had a crush on her, and this amazing synchronicity (since he was ten years her junior and not even ill) made us wonder if he wanted to escort her to the other side. Swans are even more spectacular when they fly away home.

MONTE: A TIGER TURNS INTO A SWAN

Amy and I have lived together since May of 1975, when I loaded an apartment full of possessions into a Ryder truck and said good-bye to my bachelor apartment on DeKalb Avenue, Brooklyn, just a few blocks from my alma mater, Brooklyn Technical High School. I had moved into the place with two shopping bags containing everything I owned besides my musical equipment. I had rented it a couple of years before, and doing so marked the end of seven hard years of homelessness.

My apartment had been on the top floor of an historic brownstone that I rented from a very nice African American family who lived on the floors below me. I don't know what they ended up doing with the place after all of the "improvements" I made to it.

I covered the domed ceiling of the living room with multicolored glitter, troweled spackle onto the walls of the kitchen and peaked it up like cake frosting, and then spray painted it and all of the semilethal spackle points bright gold. Then I painted the walls of the bedroom flat black and the ceiling midnight blue, both of which helped the blacked-out window shade keep out the light and enable me to sleep during the daytime when my musician's nightlife interfered with my bill-paying day job. At the time, I was the traffic manager for a hi-fi speaker company on nearby Taffee Place called Ohm Acoustics, a fancy job title meaning that I loaded tractor trailers with boxes of heavy wooden speakers every day.

My apartment was just a few blocks past Amy's former apartment above the coffee shop, which she had shared with Rupert Smith, across from the gates of Pratt Institute. Rupert turned us both on to astrology before going on to make prints for Andy Warhol.

I could not leave my first apartment without reflecting thankfully on the lessons I had learned there. I had gone from being homeless to being a low-level executive, and I was feeling good about myself again, fully emerged from the misery of poverty and self-doubt. It was not just the job and the money, though they certainly helped. I included in my grateful prayer the weekly lessons I received from Self-Realization Fellowship, the organization that is the legacy of Paramahansa Yogananda (*Parama* means "divine" and *hansa* means "swan" and refers to the mythical swan whose powers of discrimination were so acute that it could pick a drop of milk out of a lake. *Yoga* means "union," and *ananda* means "bliss." The life and teachings of this divine swan had certainly helped me find my blissful union!)

I made my bedroom closet into a meditation room and spent many happy hours there alone in Yogananda's own Kriya Yoga–style bliss. Try as I might, I cannot remember where in my apartment I put my clothes, though I think it was in the very large bathroom! However, since my desire for order in life transformed me into something of a neat freak, my place was always neat and clean.

Yogananda, who died in 1952, struck me as a truly spiritual person, and almost everyone I like turns out to have been somewhat influenced by his teachings, too. However, that was as close as I ever came to "having a guru." Amy and I have always been the kind of people for whom Shakespeare's admonition to "Put not thy faith in Princes" easily extended to the following of gurus.

Although we are swans, we are both fiercely independent and prize our ability to invent original solutions to any challenges, whether they be personal, social, artistic, or business related. It is easy to see that a union of strong, independent people creates a strong, independent union. I could never understand why so many men had a hard time with women who were fully and beautifully themselves in all their feminine strength and glory. I find that incredibly sexy about Amy, almost as sexy as she looks, sounds, and smells. I love knowing that I can depend on her for brilliantly creative and totally honest advice. There is a lot of Tiger in these two Swans and it feels divine!

CHAPTER TWO

Finding Love with Someone You Like:
Improving an Existing Relationship

If you are already with someone you like, congratulations! You are way ahead of the game, or at least we hope you are way ahead of the games that some people play to meet and be with someone they like. To find out, you can use our handy "How *Not* to Find Your Soul Mate Checklist" on page 48.

If you are relatively game-free, then double congratulations! This may be The Big One! You can use our "How to Grow a Soul Mate Checklist" on page 73 to keep you and your potential Soul Mate on the straight and narrow path to an enchanted relationship.

If you recognize yourself or your partner in more than a couple of these twelve "Do Not" checkpoints, don't despair. Instead, congratulate yourself for being so aware; many people don't bother. Be as kind to yourself as you would be to a child, and take some time alone to consider what needs to be done. Be equally kind to your partner as you lovingly explain what you now see and what you now know needs to happen to continue the glorious unfolding of your potentially legendary love affair.

If you discover that either or both of you aren't willing to improve your relationship, it might be time to put this book down for a while and take a very serious look at yourself and your partner. You can keep an okay romance going as long as you choose, but if you're looking for a life-transforming, enchanted relationship, you just can't settle for anyone who merely keeps you from being alone or who only satisfies your present definition of fun or great sex. You deserve to find and have what is the very best for *you*. However, you may eventually find that this is a relationship that is going nowhere you want to go. If you do, do not be hard on yourself. Perhaps you just needed to suffer a bit more so that you could finally learn what it is that you like, need, and deserve.

> **Secret: Duality is the central organizing principle of our reality.** We cannot know what light is unless we know darkness. We cannot know the meaning of sweet without knowing the meaning of sour. It follows that we cannot know what we like without also experiencing that which we do not like.

CHAPTER THREE

Spiritual Sex

Secret: XOX—Kisses and hugs are very important. Physical touch is the healing catalyst that allows your souls to connect and become one. Sex is one of the highest forms of expression when combined with true love. It is heightened and enlightened by mutual intimacy, trust, and joyful commitment. Without love, sex becomes just another way we avoid feeling empty. Real love is exciting because the two of you care so much about each other and want to show it in every way.

As you probably know, "Vive la difference" is a French expression meaning, "Long live the difference," which celebrates the difference between men and women. The most obvious difference is the glorious, mysterious, and overwhelming matter of sex. Don't feel bad if your own relationship looks less intense than ours. We've practiced a lot! Instead, please use the rest of *Love, Light, and Laughter* to create your own enchanted romance.

One of the nicest things about living and working together producing this book and the rest of our "children" is that we have so much time to spend sharing our innermost thoughts. Our constant proximity gives us incredible intimacy and safety, where we can be our truest selves.

We love our lives. That does not mean we have no problems. It means that we love the work that we do as author and artist, we love where we live, we love our pets, our friends and family, our creativity, and we are crazy about each other! This is a powerful energy—to love your life—and one manifestation of this celebratory feeling is spiritual sex.

AMY: SPIRITUAL SEX

For me, as a woman, my sexual desire really is profoundly affected by love, light, and laughter. It is one of the reasons that we chose the name we did for this, our most intimate book.

It is my way of describing how my emotional, mental, and spiritual levels merge with the physicality of sex to make up what we call spiritual sex. Monte responds to me on all these levels and adores me for who I am in a total way, not just physically. I think being with someone with whom they can comfortably share their deepest feelings turns most women on. Where there is no lying or pretending, we can act naturally and reveal our sexuality and ourselves without being afraid that we will be judged or misunderstood. That authenticity creates an ever-expanding openness between lovers and, afterward, a truly profound and intimate relationship.

Above all else, I think women want tenderness, affection, and understanding. There are more than a few males who possess all of these traits, but if a woman cannot find one, she should do her best to acquire these traits herself so that the men out there blessed with them see themselves in her. By knowing what we hunger for, we can reject what's inadequate and recognize the real thing when it comes along. It will come along!

When Soul Mates have spiritual sex, the excitement and attraction isn't centered in the sexual organs. Rather, we make the whole body a site for the erotic, by always giving each other a very spirited and spiritual massage before, during, and after. When you are with your Soul Mate, the act of sex produces deep intuitive communication, fondness, and fulfillment. It is like two spirits becoming one spirit; it is two worlds becoming one world. Spiritual sex is a ritual that celebrates all that reinforces love, light, and laughter in your relationship. It is a fun way, to put it mildly, to dynamically merge with the wild, pure life force of Nature.

Intimacies of Enchantment: Try These!

- Tenderly hug and kiss each other many times during each day.
- Speak in your own secret language.
- Put your foreheads together and stare into each other's eyes.
- Read aloud to each other.
- Create, share, and remember special times together.
- Tell each other about the characteristics you love about each other.
- Trust each other's judgment, both logical and intuitive.

- Give because you want to give.
- Have scents and aromas that remind you of your love and the chapters of your life together.
- Massage each other every day, not just on occasions.
- Speak and listen from your heart as well as your head.

Male and Female Energy

Though male and female energies are opposites in many ways, together they complement each other and naturally balance out to form a unity. In a successful relationship, two souls coming together create a unity.

Each of us has the dynamic forces of female and male, what the Chinese call *yin* and *yang*, within us. When we understand their cosmic dance together, we can achieve harmony in our bodies, minds, and spirits, and also in our relationships.

The following is a list of key words that might be attributed to "male" or "female" in order to give a greater insight into the qualities that govern our lives, personalities, and partnerships.

FEMALE	MALE
Right brain hemisphere	Left brain hemisphere
Left side of your body	Right side of your body
Receptive	Active
Gentle	Aggressive
Softer	Harder
Expansive	Compacted
Dark	Light
The Moon	The Sun
Diffusion	Fusion
Maternal	Paternal
Psychological	Physical
Inward	Outward
Intuitive	Rational

These male and female energies are constantly striving to find balance, both within and without. Your committed partner will manifest those opposite-sex aspects of yourself that you conceal, either consciously or unconsciously. In other words, if you are a heterosexual woman, the man you have as a partner and the way you treat him represent how you feel about the male aspects of your own personality. Likewise, if you are a man, the woman in your life and the way you treat her manifest how you feel about the feminine aspects within you.

This is not psychobabble; it is the truth as we know it in our relationship. Even before we met, each of us had already embraced those aspects of our personality opposite to our sex. We believe that is why we were able to recognize in each other the perfect complement.

Sex and the Spirit

The male/female balancing principle forms the philosophical foundation for great teachers throughout history, including Jesus, Buddha, Confucius, Lao-tzu, and Mohammed, though you might not know that by the way some adherents of these masters have treated women from the time those masters walked the earth until today.

The influence that centuries of male-dominated religions have had on all of us can be easily seen in just how we use words. For most people, the word *God* invokes the image of an all-seeing, all-knowing, all-powerful Supreme Being, while the word *Goddess* implies a quaint myth of antiquity, irrelevant to our everyday experience.

Growing up in a culture dominated by men from God on down has produced an insidious level of cultural conditioning that's scarcely visible even to most women. The belief that "Man was created in God's image" leaves many women feeling uneasy and resentful. Men would not dream of allowing a woman-dominant government to tell them what they could or could not do with their bodies, their lives, or their children's lives. Yet this is the daily experience for most of the world's female population.

It should be remembered that until the twentieth century, women were not allowed to vote in the United States of America and were in fact legally regarded as the property of their husbands. Far worse is how billions of women around the world live under severe repression, not much better than that suffered by women in the Dark Ages. Of most recent fame are the appalling circumstances of Taliban rule in Afghanistan, where women could not uncover their faces or leave home unescorted by a male relative. Less well known, perhaps, are cases in India of disgruntled husbands setting their wives on fire for supplying insufficient dowry in arranged marriages.

Male fear of female power is a personal and global tragedy. The wounded children of wounded, unequal unions mandated by unimaginative religious practice everywhere have carried a legacy of misery from ancient times until today. In fact, as we wrote in the companion book to our relationship oracle, *The Oracle of The Goddess,* "The problems that now threaten our very survival as a species may well be the cumulative result of many centuries of war fought, not between nations, but between the sexes."

Soul Mates manifest the best of their sex and spirit combined. The two of us have used our art and words to produce our series of oracles that help us all remember the ancient connection between the worship of God/dess and the art of divination, or prophecy.

The worship of both the Great Mother Goddess or God the Father and the desire to predict the future are as inseparable today as they were when woman first conceived of a Supreme Creative Force. The Judeo-Christian Bible is based on prophecies and their fulfillment; Mohammed is also known as the Prophet; and the immense population of China relies on the philosophies of Confucianism and Taoism as the basis for their ethical and legal systems, both of which are based on the I Ching, or Book of Changes, the oldest oracle system known.

The conception of a male Supreme Being found in these and other patriarchal religions so permeates nearly every aspect of contemporary culture that it's easy to assume that things have never been different. Yet there is growing evidence that the concept of the Supreme Being as a male may be a relatively recent development. In the past quarter century, scholars from fields such as archaeology, history, and theology have done research and reinterpretation of the concept of one male God. Two very accessible and informative classics on this subject are *When God Was a Woman* by Merlin Stone and *The Chalice and the Blade* by Riane Eisler.

There is much in the teachings of the founders of the patriarchal religions that is the equal in goodness and power to the teaching of The Goddess. However, much suffering and the deaths of countless millions could have been avoided had the proponents of the various patriarchal religions not decided to wage the first and bloodiest "brand-name war" to ensure that theirs was the only religion allowed.

As we have all unfortunately seen firsthand here in the twenty-first century, the fanatical proselytizers of patriarchal religions have always made it their business to erase all women's rights. In the Dark Ages, a time we are only now really starting to emerge from globally, early Christians used violence to stop the worship of The Goddess, Mother Nature, and natural energies, especially sexual energies, by branding them as evil and pagan (from the Latin, *pagus,* meaning "country"). These cultural assassins invented the Devil, the idea of an everlasting Hell, the living Hell of the

Inquisition, justified the slaughter of "non-believers," and made acceptable the persecution of witches and midwives that persists to this day.

Yet even the sternest Inquisitor could not eradicate the ancient ways of the country dwellers, whose lives required them to keep in touch with Mother Nature's rhythms, cycles, and teachings. The old ways of The Goddess took refuge in privately practiced midwifery, herbal healers, witchcraft, the tarot cards, astrology, and alchemy. All the practitioners of these ancient arts faced death for trying to keep the knowledge alive. We two are honored to continue the unbroken chain of loving wisdom and guidance.

To include and still control women in these new patriarchal religions, the "mothers" of their founders were made semidivine. Women also suffered from inhuman glorification as romantic objects. In truth, everyday life for women became anything but romantic. Because women had been considered earthly manifestations of The Goddess Herself, men used the laws of their new creed to recast themselves as the arbiters of faith and power, and to send women's power to the dark downstairs.

By denying spiritual equality between women and men, alienating people from their sense of unity with the divine in themselves and in Nature, and violently suppressing all studies and teachings that did not agree with their dogma, the patriarchal religions brought on the same Dark Ages that we're still emerging from today.

The phrase we used a few paragraphs back, "when woman first conceived of a Supreme Creative Force," was employed purposefully because we know it sounds presumptuous, even to most women. But substitute the word *man* for *woman,* and no one will bat an eye. You may just think it a literary convenience, but the practice of using an inclusive male pronoun reinforces the culturally subordinate position of women. Language matters. It is symbolic of woman's plight today. This and innumerable other daily reminders have helped to rob generations of women of their birthright as truly equal partners in the world with men.

Even though we may seem strident here, and even though we have already championed women's rights through our *Oracle of The Goddess, Gifts of The Goddess Affirmation Cards,* and our first Goddess project, *Goddess Guide Me,* we believe with all of our hearts that all the Gods and Goddesses ever worshiped are merely symbols of the un-nameable Force that created and continues to create everything. To impose a gender on It makes It more comprehensible and accessible. We are all children of these same loving Parents.

CHAPTER FOUR

Loving Children

In legal English, your children are referred to as your "issue," a wonderful synchronicity because the issue of children can make or break any relationship. It is a fact that issues about money and children are two of the biggest reasons that people have difficult relationships and even get divorced. One obvious solution to this problem is if you are not prepared emotionally, mentally, and financially to get married or to have children, then don't do either.

For many people, this advice comes too late but they should not despair. Many if not all of the secrets and lessons of *Love, Light, and Laughter,* especially the ones that help you to become yourself fully, are directly applicable to helping you be a better parent, whether or not you have romantic love in your life and whether or not the child in your care is biologically yours. Thanks to changes in science, social mores, and the rules of adoption, many people who have the overwhelming desire and the resources on all levels to have a child are now able to do so, even if they have previously lived alone. Some people have child rearing foisted upon them by unfortunate circumstances beyond their control, but they have the desire to do right by the children. No matter what your circumstances, if you are a single parent, it is especially important that you strive to balance the female and male forces inside of you as we described in the previous chapter.

We have great compassion for anyone who is caring for children and is either a single parent or someone in a difficult relationship. Both of us were raised to some degree in single-parent homes and we know how challenging this is for all concerned. As we said, Amy lost her father when she was seventeen and Monte was, from the age of twelve, raised by his aunt and mother

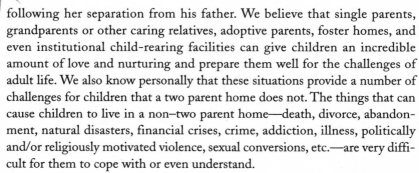

following her separation from his father. We believe that single parents, grandparents or other caring relatives, adoptive parents, foster homes, and even institutional child-rearing facilities can give children an incredible amount of love and nurturing and prepare them well for the challenges of adult life. We also know personally that these situations provide a number of challenges for children that a two parent home does not. The things that can cause children to live in a non–two parent home—death, divorce, abandonment, natural disasters, financial crises, crime, addiction, illness, politically and/or religiously motivated violence, sexual conversions, etc.—are very difficult for them to cope with or even understand.

However, as the German philosopher Friedrich Nietzsche (1844–1900) wrote, "What does not destroy [us] makes [us] stronger." Our parents and caring relatives became stronger by rising to the challenge of rearing us and our siblings after death and divorce tore their lives apart for a while. The two of us are stronger because of our early exposure to the hardships of life, but I think that everyone would prefer not to see any children exposed to the kind of suffering that can be prevented with a little forethought.

It is with that goal in mind that we say that the best thing that can happen to a child is to be born into an enchanted relationship. Soul Mates are very childlike and therefore can easily relate well to their children. They know how to relate well to other people and to put the needs of those they love ahead of their own. If your biological clock is winding down and you want to bring a child into your life before you find your enchanted relationship, that is your choice. Just make sure that you are not seeking to mold and influence a young life as a substitute for working on yourself. If you are working on yourself, you will be a fine parent.

The worst thing that can happen to a child is not divorce, though all children wish that their parents were Soul Mates or at least acted like it. Certainly, one of the worst things that can happen to children is to have their parents not be able to love or take care of them because they are not capable of doing so. Even worse is when their parents do not love them or take care of them because they simply do not want to do so. However, in our opinion, the worst thing that can happen to a child is to be abandoned or otherwise abused. It is a tragedy for all of us when one or both of a child's parents or the person responsible for giving them care abuses them verbally, emotionally, or sexually, or allows someone else to do so. Every parent worthy of the name must take this threat to his or her children as seriously as possible. If not, your children may spend many years getting over what they have suffered.

We beg everyone to not let your relationship advance to the point of engagement and marriage without both of you agreeing firmly on whether and when to have children. It is our most sincere hope that, in some small way, what we are sharing in the pages of *Love, Light, and Laugher* will contribute to a world where people form better marriages and unions, which will result in wanted, loved children.

Rearing children is an incredibly hard and important job. For those of us lucky enough to live in countries with ready access to many forms of contraception, there is no excuse for having children by accident. It isn't fair to the child, to the parent, or to the society having to pick up the pieces. Making a baby should never be done with a stranger or on a one-night stand. It should never be undertaken to "save" a relationship, to make your partner happy, to continue a family name, to make one's relatives proud, to have little people to help with the business of daily life, to have someone who *totally* loves and needs you, or to get more taxpayer money for increasing your brood. Ideally, children should only be born to Soul Mates willing to commit their lives and their relationship and their love to the welfare of their issue.

Though this may sound contradictory, we still believe that you should put your relationship first and the child or children close seconds. If you put your child first, there is no way to preserve the quality of your relationship, and the consequent wear and tear will eventually hurt your child. Your child wants happy parents who love each other. Period. Children can thrive being second in importance to their parents' relationship if their parents are Soul Mates and act like it.

We have had many people come up to us and whisper that they love their children, but they wish they had not had any. Add to those unhappy souls the folks who lack the emotional resources to even care for a cat, who wind up with one child or several. When you consider the children of these people, you can answer the question, "Why are there so many crazy, suffering people in the world?" Troubled parents produce troubled children, period.

We are often asked if we could have created the same incredible partnership if we had chosen to have children, and we have to answer no. The idea that children prevent you from having a great relationship is not true for everyone, but it was true for *us* and that is the point. You have to be true to yourself and, if you are with the right person, you can both make the incredibly important decision as to whether or not to have children based on what is best for your relationship, for each other's peace of mind, and for what you want to do with your life separately and together. That is what we did, and we have never regretted our mutual decision for a minute. Would we have stayed

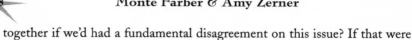

together if we'd had a fundamental disagreement on this issue? If that were the case, we would not have been true Soul Mates.

Our enchanted marriage has thrived even under the tremendous pressures involved with producing and marketing—what we like to think of as nurturing—our art, books, divination systems, ancillary products, and projects—you know, our "children," as we are fond of calling them. We have no biological children, only our beloved nephews Erik and Rune Lind, their Soul Mates, Karen Petit and Heather Steele, and our beloved niece, Sarah Zerner. We consciously decided that our creative work and our temperaments made having children ourselves something we could not manage along with our other life goals, especially for the sake of the children we might not do right by.

We knew full well that we would disappoint some family members by not having children. Being childless by choice requires the ability to stand up to the expectations and prejudices of others, especially your close family. I did not want to deprive my parents of the pleasure of grandchildren, but I know I did. Since we lived with Amy's mother, everyone told us that we had a built-in baby-sitter, but we did not want to impose that onto Jessie no matter how much she loved children. Jessie's own mother, Amy's grandmother, Rena, always said that we were obviously two people who should stay childless. And from outside the family came further reinforcement, from our friend Cheryl Lee Terry, the brilliant and accurate numerologist for many big magazines, who informed us that ours were the numbers of people who should definitely not have children.

Our decision about parenthood has always seemed to threaten the many people who wish that they, too, had had the courage to be childless by choice. We chose to be childless because we knew that fulfilling our mission in life would leave little time for a child's many important needs. We also believed and still believe that the world is full of real dangers to the people who are now inheriting it, dangers to which we did not want to expose a child. That is why we feel that only the finest, most dedicated, and well-equipped parental Soul Mates should have children. It's finally such a private and important choice.

We empathize as much as we can with those who had children but wish they hadn't, but we cannot abide hearing someone say that our marriage works only because we are childless. In fact, one of the main reasons we created our "children" is to be able to love and play with them, just like every good parent should. Of course, our children make money for us, a radical departure from the human kind! The reason our marriage works is, to a large degree, *because* of all of our "children," and all parents worthy of the name should be able to say the same.

Through the years we have learned much from observing and talking with our friends who have children. Here are ten simple ways to keep the enchantment in your relationship when you become more than two.

- Make time for each other. Hire a baby-sitter. If you can't hire a baby-sitter, get up early or stay up late. Talk to each other.

- Laugh together. Watch funny movies or tell each other jokes or reminisce about family stories.

- Let your kids see you being affectionate with each other. (Propriety is propriety and everybody's line is different. You know where yours is.) Letting kids see you hug and hear you say, "I love you," to each other will add to their own well-being and chances of having an enchanted relationship.

- Even when your kids are little, try for some activities together as a family. Maybe it's reading aloud with the whole family, not just one parent and one child at bedtime as we understand is more common. Maybe it's taking a walk around the block after dinner. We're told you can hold hands while pushing a stroller.

- Never use your children as an excuse for not working on yourself. Your children are part of your spiritual path.

- Never blame your partner for your kids' behavior. Work hard at staying on the same page with issues of discipline, expectations, and everyday behavior. Talk to each other. If you can't agree, there's no shame in seeking help.

- Play with your children, alone or together. Children have a way of being their parents' teachers, especially when it comes to having a playful attitude.

- Make sure you each get some alone time. Look out for each other this way.

- Remember love is not a zero-sum game. The more you share with your partner and your children, the more you have to share.

- Hint: You can use the tools in part 2 of this book to shed light on your family relationship and your interaction with your children as well as on your partnership.

CHAPTER FIVE

Unrequited Love

We, the Enchanted (childless) Couple, are equal opportunity Cupids. *Love, Light, and Laughter* is meant for everyone desirous of finding their Soul Mate, and that includes same sex partnerships and couples dealing with differences of age, race, ethnic background, social status, religion, customs, traditions, and a whole host of other disparities.

We believe that if any relationship can survive the "How *Not* to Find Your Soulmate Checklist" (see page 48), that is, by working on yourselves and your relationship according to the advice in our "How to Grow a Soul Mate Checklist" (see page 73), then the challenges mentioned above won't stop you, even if your family, friends, and perfect strangers may try to do so. Soul Mates give each other support in good times and bad, so you will get through the tough times.

However, there are situations that will completely derail your search for an enchanted relationship. If you're being abused by a partner, you have *not* found your Soul Mate. If you are not in an abusive relationship, you can either skip the rest of this chapter or read it and feel very fortunate. Dealing with abuse fully is beyond the scope of this book. However, on the chance that you're in an abusive relationship and have gotten this far in our book, you're at least somewhat receptive to what we have to say. So here's our opinion of what you should do.

Abuse Is Not Something You Can Live With

If you, your children, or anyone in your family is being abused, including your pets (those who abuse pets are very likely to exhibit sociopathic behavior toward people), you are in a living hell, not in a relationship, no matter what you think or how much you want to deny it. If you are in an abusive relationship, get help. If professional help and counseling fails to make things substantially better, get out. Period. Do not give your abuser any more chances to harm you or your family, no matter how many apologies, promises, and gifts you receive. Just leave. Even if it looks to you like you cannot get out, call your nearest battered women's shelter, hospital, police department, or other professional organization devoted to helping you and the many other people in your situation escape from your self-created prison. You are in deeper trouble than you know because you are being abused and therefore cannot think straight. It is not your fault, but it is a fact.

Even if you have bought into your abuser's lies about how the abuse is your fault or the fault of your children, *you must assume that you are not thinking straight* and leave. Leave now! Even if you think you still love your abuser, you have to get away, *now*. Remember how we all need to be alone sometimes? For you, that time is now. When you are in a peaceful environment, you will realize that abuse cancels out love. They cannot exist together, just like you cannot live with someone who is abusing you, your children, or anyone, including himself or herself.

Yes, it is true that you got yourself into your situation, but do not dwell on how badly you screwed up. Punishing yourself gave you the low self-esteem that got you into an abusive situation in the first place. The good news is that you can get yourself out of your nightmare now, no matter how impossible that may seem. You need professional help to help you see what is really going on.

There is a strong chance that, with professional help, you will come to realize that your family also suffered the ravages of abuse when you were a child. It is common that abusive people and their victims accept abuse because it was what they learned that family was all about. Please, please, please realize that an abusive relationship is not normal. It can only get worse if you stick around and try to change it. Remember, you cannot change anyone, nor can you expect him to change if he obviously does not want to. If you do not want to be maimed or die or ruin the lives of your children, get professional help and get out.

If you are the abuser of your partner, your children, or even yourself, with alcohol, drugs, or self-destructive behaviors, you have to realize that you are sick and need to go to the doctor. Giving in to your compulsions will not really help you to feel better. You have to get professional help on the physical plane, in reality, or you are only delaying your inevitable ruin. Altering your mood by overeating, binging and purging, drinking, drugging, practicing compulsive or unsafe sex, lying, risk-taking, cheating, or doing anything other than getting help and getting to the root of your real problems is not going to free you from your living hell.

Sometimes You Just Have to Move On

If you are with someone you like, and she makes it clear by her words or actions that she does not like you, you have a choice. As reality dawns, you can stay calm and find out what the trouble is. If it is something that can be worked on and you are *both* willing to give it a try, then we are back to congratulations and your relationship will be the better for it. If *both* of you are not willing to try to work things out, then you have to move on to your second choice, which is to leave what you thought was *the* relationship, spend some time alone or with friends, family, or spiritual advisors, and see what you can learn from this painful situation so you won't have to repeat it.

Why waste your time staying with someone obviously wrong for you? Even if you fear being alone, poorer, losing friends and social standing, depriving your children of a caregiver, the unknown, we sincerely doubt that you should stay together. When you are working on yourself and your self-esteem and want an enchanted relationship, you cannot move forward unless you leave where you were and make a space in your life for new possibilities. Life is short, and you do not have time to waste. Cut your losses and move on.

In rare instances, people who go through this or other kinds of breakups do get back together. We know two such rare couples personally. Barry Shapiro, a dear friend of both of us separately before we met, and his wife, Patricia Miles, divorced and have now reconciled and gotten back together. And two of our closest friends, Audrey Flack and her husband, Bob Marcus, were high school sweethearts who married other people but divorced them and found each other again in true enchanted storybook fashion.

However, for your own good, you are much better off assuming the relationship is over. The only thing that is going to effect that kind of miracle is time and solitary effort. If your relationship really is worth saving, you still have to let it go completely and explore as many options available to you as you can. Otherwise, you will be a wounded person trying to patch up a wounded relationship with someone who may very well not like you or himself enough to avoid hurting you even more next time. Soul Mates do not cause each other that kind of pain, no matter what anyone says. Be kind to your "enchanted self," also known as the child within you, and make a clean break for everybody's sake. Your enchanted self is the uncorrupted, pure, and open part of you receptive to unlimited possibilities. Let it lead you back to the path of light and laughter, if love is not in the picture right now. You should always love yourself, even if it seems you have wasted your time. At least you did not hurt anyone but yourself.

Fooling Around Is Neither Fun nor Funny

If the game you are playing involves a married person, or a person committed to someone else, be very, very careful. You are playing a dangerous game that has the potential to hurt you more than anyone else involved. The Golden Rule of the world's religions is, "Do unto others as you would have them do unto you," and it did not get to be the Golden Rule by not being true. The word *karma* is the Hindu word describing the actions we take and the actions that come back at us as a result of those actions, positive or negative. The modern expression of this is, "What goes around, comes around."

If the person you are with is willing to cheat on someone she supposedly used to love or like, just as she supposedly loves or likes you, then what makes you think that she wouldn't be willing to do the same thing to you? Some people enjoy the hunt for their Soul Mate more than actually finding one. They become addicted to the process; they are in love with the idea of falling and being in love.

If you team up with your lover to bring pain to another person, you must be willing to endure the consequences of your actions. Unless you are with someone actually and actively separating from their previous relationship, not just talking about it, there is no way that your relationship can survive the test of our two checklists. If you cannot see this, consider if you're so desperate to have a relationship that you are willing to blind yourself and go against what you know is right. Where can that lead but to heartbreak and pain?

Whatever you give out will come back to you. Love, and you will receive love in return. Exude light by being a kind, positive, and caring person, and illumination will be your reward. Laugh, and you will attract congeniality from others.

Try your best to understand hostility, negativity, fear, and anger from within you. These emotions generally come from low self-esteem. We don't believe in repressing these feelings, but in acknowledging them and patiently affirming positive thoughts so as not to make our systems or our lives toxic.

Secret: Observe how your habitual thoughts affect your life. It is the nature of habits to rule us unless we first become aware that they are habits, examine the events that gave rise to them, and become aware of how they actively influence us. The only way to eliminate a habit is through patient awareness and the belief that your life will change for the better if you stop acting or thinking in the old habitual way.

AMY: FIGHTING FAIR

Monte and I share everything. We share truth. We share our joys and accomplishments, the beauty of art, sorrow, disappointment, and all of our observations, insights, and secrets. We are sincerely interested in each other on a deep level and have a great deal of affection, tenderness, and respect for each other. Our life is rich because we genuinely communicate and participate in each other's self-acceptance. Our relationship is never dull, because we are always finding out how each other feels and working through our inner worlds, which provides an atmosphere for change, growth, and creativity.

People ask us if we fight. Of course! The process of standing up for an idea or confronting issues, or "clearing the air," is a natural and healthy part of any relationship. I would be suspicious of couples who say they never fight. But there are different ways of fighting; there is "dirty" fighting, and there is "fair" fighting. To me, it's "dirty" of you to say things that hurt, humiliate, or exploit another's feelings, secrets, or vulnerabilities.

Fair fighting is facing real issues or working out problems constructively. This can really deepen a relationship, which is the goal, after all. Sometimes the stress of work deadlines or finances or unrealistic demands makes people throw tantrums, but smart lovers don't take this personally. It is more like waiting for a tired baby to let off steam or finish being cranky.

We both know that there are usually clues before a confrontation that we've learned to recognize. That is why we take preventive measures to reduce our stress: exercise, massage, time out for tea, breathing, cuddling, or a nap. All help to center and calm us so that we can feel strong to listen and communicate with love and understanding. At the same time, we try to avoid irritations that can exacerbate stress, like caffeine, alcohol, lack of sleep, toxic thoughts, and toxic people.

Of course, laughter is always the best medicine and we often kid each other out of our bad moods. Humor always helps to break down our defenses and to accept our quirks and perceived mistakes. We all can be overly self-critical because of past and present mistakes. True love can make us more secure and accepting of personality differences and tensions, our strengths as well as our weaknesses. If we say the truth in a loving way we can help the other person to overcome conflicts within themselves and see the issues more clearly.

If humor doesn't work, you will always be better off affirming your partner's feelings, rather than ordering him to see your side of the situation, unless he's in a dangerous rage. It is also important to not show anger yourself, no matter how upset you might be. Though it is natural to get upset to see someone you love in such a state, you must have faith that if she lets her feelings out for both of you to witness, you will eventually come to a better understanding of what buttons have been pushed and why. It is one manifestation of what the Buddhists call "being mindful." Mindfulness gives you an advantage on things, instead of a tug into the torrent of your own emotions. If you argue, diminish, or, worst of all, mock your partner's feelings, you can expect nothing but pain and suffering for the both of you. Soul Mates are always trying their best to be there for each other.

The great thing about being with someone you love is that if you can remember that life is short and there are no guarantees, you can recover your equilibrium fairly quickly by realizing how lucky you are just to have your health and to be with the person you love. That realization has kept us going through the hard times that confront even an enchanted couple.

Monte and I make a point to let each other feel comfortable to release our feelings without fear of criticism. We don't throw mistakes in each other's faces. We admire each other when we have the courage to see the truth and lessons in the situation and to face them constructively. We try to avoid misunderstandings by giving productive feedback and insights into how our feelings influence our behavior. In that way we can strengthen each other's sense of self-esteem and be alert to each other's needs. We are both very protective, caring, and mindful of our relationship.

In an authentic enchanted relationship, you take time to transform suffering and pain into happiness. When we are enchanted, we can accept our partner's love as well as give our own; we can be cared for as well as give care; we can learn as well as teach; we can depend on each other as well as be independent enough to know our own minds and bodies. Being enchanted opens us to the creativity and spirituality working through us, and keeps us open to our partner, each contributing to the other's dreams, hopes, desires, and ultimate joy.

CHAPTER SIX

How *Not* to Find Your Soul Mate

This is one of the most important chapters in *Love, Light, and Laughter*. If you learn the lessons of this chapter, you are almost guaranteed to have healthy, enchanted relationships, and you may very well meet your Soul Mate. If you do not, nothing short of a miracle can help you. Don't just take our word for it.

MONTE: LISTEN TO THE NYPD

Believe it or not, one of the main reasons for my having one of the best marriages that this world has ever seen is something that my father and his fellow NYPD tough-guy cop friends taught me as a child. Like most of the men of that time, my father's fellow officers defined themselves by how strong they were. Practically every man, no matter how sensitive he was inside, walked around like he was keeping a troubling secret and would rather fight you than talk to you about what was bothering him. Imagine a whole world populated by legions of James Cagney, Humphrey Bogart, and George Raft wanna-bes (if you are too young to know who they are, rent their movies).

I was privileged to have the 74th Police Precinct in Prospect Park as both my playground and a safe haven from the neighborhood bullies. I was big for my age but sensitive and psychic, though I didn't realize it at the time. Growing up there and then was for me a dark, bewilderingly cruel, and frightening experience. I thought that there was something wrong with me because the other guys all acted so tough. One day, I got up the nerve to ask my father's colleagues, "Are you ever afraid, even though you are a policeman?"

They took this question very seriously and all agreed that the call they most dreaded to hear coming over their police radios was "Domestic

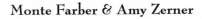

Dispute." It was amazing to me to hear that what they feared the most was when it was their job to come into a couple's home either before, during, or after there had been serious physical damage done. However, these very tough guys did not fear abusive husbands and boyfriends, mobsters, street gangs, or riots; they were afraid of housewives.

"You come in and the guy's just bouncing her off the wall. She's all banged up so you pull them apart. There's a few broads who just love beating up their husbands, but it's usually the guy who's the jerk and we have to 'restrain' him and sometimes that means we have to get pretty rough with the guy. That's when in she runs and stabs one of us with a kitchen knife! Here she is, bleeding, teeth knocked out, eyes swelling shut, but she's defending her man, the guy that just mopped the floor with her! These women marry these guys thinking that they're going to change them. Listen, Monte, you can't change anyone. It's hard enough to change yourself!"

One of the things that has saved my life many times is that I know the truth when I hear it. You can't change anyone. It's hard enough to change yourself. That was, is, and always will be the truth.

In our case, since the day we met, neither of us wanted to change each other. It was obvious to each of us that we were both fully engaged in self-discovery and self-improvement. As we got to know each other better, we made our relationship a safe place for either of us to seek the other's help in effecting personal change, but only if help was asked for.

> **Secret: You can only change yourself; you cannot change anyone else.** You can, however, make sure you get involved with a person who desires change for the better. Devoting time to self-improvement or study will always enable you to improve your situation. The desire to grow is one of our most basic needs.

If you do not want to meet your Soul Mate, if you do not want to have an enchanted relationship, if you do not want to have even a decent friendship, then keep expecting to change the other person, especially your romantic partner, especially when it is obvious that they do not want to change or be changed.

The How *Not* to Find Your Soul Mate Checklist

We are often surprised to hear people describe themselves as looking to get married. It is as silly to us as saying you're looking to make a hundred million dollars; it can happen, but there is a lot that has to happen first.

These people let their desperation and anticipatory fears get the better of them. After only a date or two, they start talking to their friends about whether or not they are going to marry this person. Sadly, they do not see how unrealistic and self-defeating this kind of behavior is. Even if these musings are never revealed to anyone, that hurry-up kind of attitude can kill a relationship in its early stages, unless you happen to have found someone also desperate to get married. Even then, I would not give such a marriage a good chance of becoming enchanted. Keep your eye on the prize of building a great relationship founded on caring, thoughtfulness, friendship, and mutual support, and love, marriage, and great sex are sure to follow.

Here is the "How *Not* to Find Your Soul Mate Checklist." On it are most of the silly, fear-based things that people do that limit opportunities to find their Soul Mate. You may want to add a few things to it, based on your own experiences.

1) ❑ Do not let anyone know how much or how little you are interested in him/her, romantically or otherwise. If he/she figures it out, deny it.

2) ❑ Do not let the topic of conversation stray away from you. Make it clear that all you think about is yourself by not paying any attention to other people's words, deeds, or body language.

3) ❑ Do not forget to be abusive, ignore everyone's feelings, complain constantly, and be critical of everyone and everything. Show that you are greedy, impossible to please, and love saying mean things about people behind their backs.

4) ❑ Do not fail to judge potential partners by your own list of must-have traits: looks, money, job, family, status, religion, size, shape, hair, color, and so forth. (You know, the list that has gotten you into your present situation dozens of times!)

5) ❑ Do not avoid talking about who you think is "hot," or about your previous marriages and romances, if any. Do not make eye contact with your date but instead look at any other attractive or important people who are anywhere near you.

6) ❑ Do not fail to act superficial, bored, and indifferent about the talents, accomplishments, and interests of your possible new Soul Mate. Show that you feel that people who are totally committed and passionate about anything are naive if not total idiots.

7) ❑ Do not apologize if you are late or for anything else, even if your actions have obviously hurt the person you supposedly love. Make sure you never, ever forgive him/her or let him/her forget any of his/her mistakes.

8) ❑ Do not like your potential Soul Mate's pets, beloved family, or close friends. Even better, make it clear that you like them a little too much.

9) ❑ Do not fail to act jealous and possessive and be sure to tell your potential Soul Mate you want to control his/her behavior and change him/her for his/her own good.

10) ❑ Do not tell the truth to your potential Soul Mate. Do not care if he/she sees you are a pathetic liar, a scheming phony, or have no idea what is real, who you are, or how you feel about anything.

11) ❑ Do not forget to mention how the two of you should get married and have children when you are on one of your first (and soon to be one of your last) dates. If you have children already, the choice is yours: either do not mention them at all or talk about nothing else.

12) ❑ Do not forget that getting drunk or otherwise stoned will make the preceding eleven "Do nots" easier, and as a bonus, will show your potential Soul Mate you are seriously troubled and trying to escape from reality!

We would be lying if we told you that we never manifested any of these behaviors before or during our courtship, and that our relationship progressed on a straight line toward enchantment. We were exploring our opportunities and our powers, just like young people have done since the human race was created, and we were sometimes a bit clumsy at it. More than a few times, it looked like we would not move closer than our fears and bad habits would allow.

Our meeting happened a long time ago. Though it is impossible for us to remember exactly what we were thinking, we can say with certainty that neither of us was looking to get married. In fact, the opposite was true. We found in each other someone unwilling to manipulate us into marriage or anything else. We did not have a laundry list of qualities we were looking for or what we could not stand in a potential boyfriend or girlfriend. We were open to the moment and were therefore able to see with our own eyes, not with the eyes of our former selves or of those who had influenced our development. The reason that we persevered and, in seven short months, decided to live together "for the summer" was that we each got a certain something out of being with each other that we knew we could not get from being with anyone else. Feeling that way about someone is the first sign that you may have met your Soul Mate!

CHAPTER SEVEN

Obstacles on the
Road to Enchantment

The biggest obstacle to your enchanted relationship is not your partner's problems and faults, your appearance, your level of income, quality of housing, education, free time, or, if you're single, the small number of decent and suitable partners "out there." The biggest problem is "in here," in you: your inner fears about yourself and life. Obstacles are outward manifestations of the fears that we have inside of us.

Living happily ever after does not mean that you will never be unhappy. Our friend Marianne Williamson, one of the brightest lights we know of, says in her book, *Return to Love*, that there are only two main paths that we can choose at any moment, love or fear. In our life together, we have always tried to use our love to help us overcome our fears and the problems caused by them. However, we will always continue to work on both our love and our fears.

> **Secret: Know that you have the power to defeat negative thinking and behavior.** Learn to understand and cope with your greatest enemy: your own fear. We have learned that living a successful life of quality and meaning does not mean that you won't react to fear, uncertainty, or rejection. What is important is how quickly you recover your equilibrium and get on with the business of living.

The three stories that follow are the stories of how we faced our dark sides. These were the greatest challenges of our life together, and they almost broke us apart. Were it not for love, light, and laughter, we would probably not be married or even alive!

AMY: PANIC NEAR NEEDLE PARK

I had my first panic attack in 1979, in New York City. That morning I had sniffed a bit of cocaine from my little brown vial, ate half a bagel with cream cheese, and went off into the day. This was an ordinary start to my day at the time. I left Monte's sister's apartment (we were sharing the rent) on West 74th Street, a couple of blocks from the little triangular area known as Needle Park back then and with good reason. It was populated with junkies and got really scary when they started fighting over drugs, which they always did. I was so oblivious that I did not associate my cocaine use with them in the slightest bit. Drugs do that to you.

I was headed across town for a haircut. I think I sniffed a little more cocaine when I got to Jean's salon. I was chatty of course, but all of a sudden, during the shampoo, I started to feel disoriented and trapped, like I couldn't breathe. I tried to tell the salon's foreign assistant that maybe I had low blood sugar and asked if could she bring me something to eat. I think they rustled up a piece of bread, but by the time I got into the chair for my haircut, the reflection of my ashen face in the mirror shocked me. My heart began pounding and I knew that I had to get out of there.

They called Monte to pick me up. Luckily, he was home and came to "rescue" me. The whole experience left me scared and confused. Was it the cocaine? Was it my heart? Was I flipping out? Was it stress? Then and there I took the experience as a sign to stop doing drugs, and I stopped—I have not since taken any drug beyond an occasional aspirin into my body. That's how profound a turning point my first panic attack was in my life. Little did I know that there were many more lessons to be learned before I licked this demon. Unfortunately, even after I stopped all drugs, the panic attacks continued.

After that first episode, I was terrified that I would be out in the world alone, on a bus or on the street, and suddenly I would start hyperventilating, sweating, and fearing the worst would happen. Phobias develop when you associate the panic attack with a specific location. For instance, if you have one while driving, or while in a department store, you fear you will again have an attack there. Luckily, I overcame my fear of hair salons, since my purple hair takes quite a few visits.

However, after my initial journeys through the nightmare world of not trusting my mind, my body, or the world to take care of me, I became preoccupied with thoughts of unexpected panic attacks. Then, of course, I would have one. Walking down the street, the sidewalk and people would start to seem unreal, my vision would become unfocused, and my heart felt like it might leap out of my chest. These attacks seemed to strike without warning, and fear would shoot through me like a bullet from a gun. I became hyper-vigilant, beset by anticipatory anxiety: when would I lose control? I was so embarrassed and confused by what was happening to me that I told very few people.

After attending a wedding where I surreptitiously took my pulse the whole time because I was in such a high level of anxiety, which, of course, caused my heart to beat rapidly, I made an appointment with my friend Carol Sigler, a nurse who had recently gotten her acupuncture license. She is a master teacher and practitioner now.

Her husband, Steve, was our Harvard-trained family doctor. He also knew acupuncture, a rarity in those days and a tribute to his bravery in the face of open hostility from the medical establishment.

I think I was one of Carol's first patients. When I lay myself down on her table, she took my pulse, felt it racing, and had to laugh because it made her feel like her heart was racing—it was thumping so hard! She turned me over and "drained my anger" with a series of needles in my back. It did calm me down. I also felt relieved to share my feelings with a professional healer. She was very empathetic and reassuring.

She sent me for some tests, including an EKG and one for mitral valve prolapse, which often mimics the same symptoms I was having. I was looking forward to finding out what was actually wrong with me, though I was concerned that something was seriously wrong with my heart. I also had a complete physical with blood tests. All the tests came back normal.

Then it must be some terrible weakness in my character, I thought, not remembering that was how I used to view the alcoholism my father had suffered from. As I continued my weekly acupuncture sessions (and my weekly panic attacks!), I became more aware of my deep feelings of insecurity. With Carol's help, I was able to reflect on how, at age twenty-eight, I had developed a habit of denying my anger and stress by setting high goals for myself in order to prove that I was "together," smart, competent, and in control, when I was actually introspective, shy, and highly sensitive. I was also a worrier, but I was so used to it that I did not realize that there was any other way to think, feel, and act.

My father's unexpected death made it difficult for me to ever feel completely safe. His many years of alcoholism culminated in a heart attack and a fatal car accident that devastated me. Deep inside myself I was expecting another frightening event. I had developed an anticipatory fight or flight response to my fears: fears about our precarious finances, about the "failures"

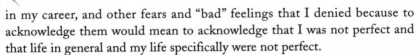

in my career, and other fears and "bad" feelings that I denied because to acknowledge them would mean to acknowledge that I was not perfect and that life in general and my life specifically were not perfect.

Instead, I felt I needed to deal with all of these pressures serenely, showing little suffering and no stressful side effects. Thus, I was repressing my true feelings, which popped out inappropriately as panic attacks. In trying to live up to the perceived expectations of others, I ignored the signs of emotional exhaustion that my body was trying to give me. I was tired, so all I needed, I rationalized, was a little boost (cocaine), so that I could pride myself in working long hours on tapestries that were not selling the way I wanted them to. As a result, I became extrasensitive to all stimuli, especially drugs.

Cocaine leads to spontaneous panic attacks and creates a racing, overstimulated heartbeat (as can aspartame and MSG). At the time of my first panic attack, my bloodstream was also probably laden with insulin from all the starches I was eating, and that aggravated my symptoms. In my healing process, I began a journey toward healthy eating habits and gradually figured out ways to deal with the high levels of anxiety that I had permitted to strain and overload me. I learned not to be ashamed of my feelings, discovered how to assert myself, and developed a better self-image. I was so motivated to get better that I was willing to take what felt to me like very frightening steps. Having read everything I could on the subject of panic attacks, I knew that it was a progressive condition and that if I hadn't gotten help, I probably would have become housebound. That, indeed, was a scary thought.

I stopped doing drugs more than a year before Monte did and this caused a lot of stress on our relationship—probably the most we have ever had to endure—as he will describe to you in a few pages.

Recovery is not easy, but hard work will pay off if you try to change your behavior. Our marriage survived this negative manifestation of my Saturn transit, something Monte will tell you about in the next section, and was actually strengthened. Now we listen more closely to our bodies and heed their warnings to rest or stop. We still have bouts of perfectionism or worry, especially about losing each other, but we no longer deny our feelings, even when they are feelings of sadness, anger, stress, or guilt.

I learned coping skills that helped me to drive a car without anxiety. I had developed a phobia about driving, an indication that my father's accident was part of the root cause of my problem. I was finally able to feel comfortable in the most intimidating situations, such as flying in airplanes or having to speak in public. I was astounded to learn that people in surveys said they were more afraid of public speaking than of their own deaths! My "attacks" per-sisted for years, but since I'd have many panic-free months, it didn't disrupt my life. I didn't let my imagination create mortifying scenarios (by the way, highly imaginative people seem to develop this disorder).

When I would have an inexplicable recurrence or develop fears of dizzi-ness or disorientation, I often reassured myself (which felt silly sometimes!) by giving myself a pinch on the cheek or a stroke of my hand! Most impor-tantly, Monte's love and understanding always made me feel safe to express my feelings.

Years later, when we would fly around the country to promote our books, I'd start to panic when the doors of the airplane were sealed shut. I knew that I could share my uneasiness with Monte and, rather then telling me that there was no sense in feeling this way, he would tell me that he felt a little funny about it, too, and it would be all right with him if I ran screaming through the cabin. Light remarks like that would help me laugh at my irra-tional thoughts.

Being the extreme Aquarius that he is, he would sometimes take it a bit too far and say that he understood perfectly well why I would feel afraid to go hurtling through the air in a metal tube, a machine made and maintained by the same hung-over, beer-swilling men who care more passionately about sports than their jobs (the same reason he feared nuclear power reactors). Seeing that that did not make me feel much better, he would try the scien-tific, logical approach and explain to me the scientific principles underlying flight but, in a strange quest to be totally truthful, he also admitted that the difference in air pressure over a curved and straight surface did not sound like something you would want to bet your life on.

What actually helped was when he reminded me that everyone on the air-plane was using their own methods of dealing with their very logical fear of flying, whether that was complete denial, rabbits' feet, or prayer. These days, flying does not bother me and I have actually successfully calmed down first-time flyers who were sitting next to us!

We also patiently worked on my stage fright. As it did with panic attacks and as it does in all aspects of our life, the language of astrology—our lan-guage of love—helped us to understand and deal with it. By understanding our different Rising Signs, Monte and I understood specific differences in our personalities and went on from there. Instead of expecting each other to be the same as each other or just like everyone else, we helped each other to explore our differences with patient understanding and mutual support. If that is not a powerful secret, I do not know what is.

Monte, being what is known in astrology as a Leo Rising, has redefined stage fright in his usual funny way. Leo is the sign of the flamboyant showman and actor, and he realized that he, too, had stage fright, but a different kind: he got scared when he *wasn't* on stage!

Though I had always admired his ability to get up in front of a crowd of people and sing, play music, lecture, or even do a stand-up comedy act without the slightest preparation, Monte made me see that people who enjoy doing those things also feel their hearts race, the flushed feeling, and the anticipatory excitement. The only difference was that Monte and these people like that feeling, in the same way that some people enjoy a roller coaster ride or a horror movie.

There is a deeper spiritual implication in all of this. If our personalities do survive our physical death, as our experience with my mother and with mediums like John Edwards and James Van Praagh seem to prove, it is possible that, at its essence, our life on Earth is a kind of roller coaster ride. Beyond earthly existence lies an unimaginable way of being. Imagine living without the fear of physical pain, without longing or suffering of any kind, especially the loss of loved ones, and without fear of death!

Understanding our Rising Signs enables us to have the kind of in-depth dialogue with each other that most people only have with a therapist. Being totally committed to working together on our problems with gentleness, patience, and loving friendship is one of the most important secrets for building the kind of strong bond we share into your own relationship. In our case, it is okay to love your therapist (and your astrologer) as much as you want!

Seriously speaking, astrology is no magic trick. It can give you and your partner a set of principles with which to understand each other and to communicate. If you don't already know astrology, you and your partner can learn it together. Astrology offers a common language the same way therapy does. I will give you a little grounding in it now and, if you are interested in learning more, you might want to try Monte's *Karma Cards: A New Age Guide to Your Future Through Astrology* or *The Enchanted Astrologer,* two of the simplest and most fun ways to get a solid grounding in astrology.

In astrology, the Rising Sign symbolizes how you interface with the world. Your Sun Sign, the one you read in a newspaper horoscope, is based on the day you were born, but your Rising Sign is based on the exact time and place you were born. The time and place of your birth determines exactly which of the 360 degrees of the Zodiac (which comes from the Greek *kykylos zodiakus,* meaning "circle of animals") is rising on the horizon at the moment of your birth, as viewed from where you are born. If you are born at sunrise, then you are a "double" sign and the daily newspaper horoscope, if it is done correctly, will be more accurate for you than for most other people. Most people aren't born at sunrise.

Knowing that I was an Aries Sun Sign actually helped me understand my panic attacks. Aries is another name for Mars, the Roman god of war, and those born under its influence are known for being very direct, aggressive, and honest. If that energy is blocked, it has to come out somewhere. The Aries personality is easily provoked into a "fight or flight" response, and they display the same type of panic that chipmunks do when something blocks their usual path. The thing that Aries people fear the most is being afraid. It is easy to see how people born during the time of Aries could be prone to panic attacks.

To make my predisposition for panic even stronger, I am a Scorpio Rising, a sign that, until the discovery of the planet Pluto in the 1930s, was also associated with, or "ruled by," the planet Mars. However, Scorpios are not fiery like Aries; their intensity is more inner and emotional. Scorpio Rising people present a deceptively calm exterior to the world while their inner passions are boundlessly deep. They are reluctant to display their feelings because they value secrecy as a way to maintain their power. They are very sensitive to ridicule. You can see that I was predisposed to having panic attacks.

One of the great benefits of astrology is that it helps you to see how to use your strengths to overcome your weaknesses. I was able to draw on my Aries bravery to fly and to speak on the radio, even when the show was being broadcast live from the center of a crowded Tacoma, Washington, shopping mall many years ago. Every time I was ready to give up and run, Monte would tell me that it was okay and that I did not have to do it. That helped a lot. Sitting next to someone so gregarious also helped because I knew that if I froze up, he would be able to take over.

I have also attended many, many openings of my art exhibits and that certainly desensitized me to crowds and public speaking, too. I am often asked to give lectures about my work and, though I never thoroughly enjoy the experience because of my shyness, I have become much more comfortable doing it.

Gradually, I was able to go on television. I started with our local public access station but soon graduated to full segments on *Alive and Wellness with Carol Martin*, a wonderful national TV talk show on the now-defunct America's Talking network. We have now also done segments on *B. Smith With Style*, a national show, *Good Day New York*, FOX TV's flagship morning show, and other TV shows in cities throughout the United States and Canada.

The biggest test of my wellness was our appearance on QVC and the Home Shopping Network (HSN), where Monte and I became the first people in history to sell tarot cards on national television. QVC is in West Chester, Pennsylvania, outside of Philadelphia, so we were able to drive there. But HSN is in Florida, so we had to fly there in order to appear in front of millions of television viewers several times during a day, grabbing power naps when we could. During this experience I had to completely confront my tendency to panic, my fear of flying, and my unease while speaking in public. I am proud to say that it was also my graduation.

Even with all of my progress, I continued to be nervous before going on the air. Often, my sleep would be disrupted, though Monte would sleepily do his best to remind me of how I had been worried the last time but had done fine. His standard line was, "When the red light on top of the TV camera goes on, you will be fine, just like you are always fine no matter how much you worry about it." My graduation came after a particularly good segment we'd done that we watched later on videotape. Monte took pleasure in pointing out that when the red light on top of the TV camera came on, I was not only all right, I did not let him get a word in edgewise! Now, I barely worry and, if I do, I use the techniques that you'll find at the end of this chapter. They have certainly helped to cure me.

Panic attacks and agoraphobia are the number one mental health problems among women and second only to drug and alcohol abuse among men. Adult children of alcoholics have a high risk of developing panic attacks. I also believe that there is a strong genetic predisposition to this condition, as well as a biochemical component. As a child, I had an unusual fear of bridges, and I also found out, in sharing all of this information with my mother, that I had been born a month late. That could certainly account for my phobias about being trapped, like on the sealed-in passenger cabin on a plane!

Many agoraphobics have one or more relatives with the same anxieties or phobias. There is a definite tendency in my family, and I believe my own healing journey gave them help and insights into their own predispositions. Now we can laugh at these "quirks." My mother and I exchanged many personal stories of her episodes, which further cemented the bond between us, since we understood each other's experience so intimately.

A lot of agoraphobics have low blood pressure, low blood sugar, and hidden food allergies. One doctor, Dr. Azim Etemadi, discovered that agoraphobics have low levels of serotonin and that they are prone to anxiety because of this.

Serotonin-building foods are walnuts, fish, eggs, and other protein-rich foods. Caffeine, starches, and alcohol are no-nos. He also prescribed L-5-Hydroxytryptophan, which helps to build serotonin. These natural approaches helped me tremendously. In my opinion, some doctors are too quick to prescribe drugs. I feel it is better to use natural remedies when possible, along with behavioral therapy. Here are some of the cognitive therapy secrets that helped me overcome my fears:

- When unwanted thoughts intrude, snap yourself back into the present moment by wearing a rubber band on your wrist and snapping it.

- Focus on something that you can touch or taste. That will distract your racing thoughts by putting your mind on something other than you and your fear.

- Go through with what you have to do, no matter how you are feeling; never retreat.

- Keep trying and you will make progress. Believe that you have the capacity to change.

- Always breathe through anticipatory fear; take a deep breath, hold it as long as you can, and let it out slowly.

- Give comfort, not criticism, to your inner child, what we call your "enchanted self." Treat yourself the way you would treat a frightened child; be the most gentle and patient parent you can imagine.

- Practice affirmations and positive imaging.

- Lighten up and laugh at yourself and, oh yes, love yourself more.

I have been free of agoraphobia and panic attacks for many years. I hope that revealing my experiences and the techniques that have helped me may serve to help others suffering from this crippling condition.

MONTE: DRUGS AND BABY BOOMERS—PRODUCTS OF OUR TIME

Amy and I were teenagers in the 1960s. Since then we have continuously maintained our commitment to the same primary goal we had before we even met: we make art that helps us and our audience experience life at its highest possible level. Unfortunately, back then, we naively believed that drugs could help us to get closer to our divine nature. Individually and as a generation, we were not just trying to get high; we were trying to get higher.

No one high on drugs can do the hard work necessary to really change the world, though that was what our generation professed to want to do. We started out thinking we were going to use drugs like the Native American shamans, but what we forgot was that those holy people endured years of training and grueling preparation before they were allowed by their teachers to enter that shadowy world. We ran into that world without so much as a beach towel to protect us, and it's a miracle that any of us survived to tell about it.

Of course, this generation accomplished a lot of great things, both because of our beliefs and in spite of them. We championed the notions of racial and sexual equality and challenged ideas about the nobility of war and fighting. Our marching and protests, which pitted me against my police sergeant father and the policemen he was in charge of on the barricades of the New York anti-war marches, did finally force Nixon and Kissinger to make an earlier end to the war in Vietnam. My father eventually apologized to me for his stance on the war. (He never apologized for throwing me out of the house.) I had started smoking marijuana after he gave me the boot. It was right after I found out that I was not going to be drafted and left school. Fast-forward to the fall of 1979 and on until July 4th, 1981, when I violated the rules of enchanted relationships and put Amy and me through the worst period of our lives. When one puts something above the relationship and the two partners start growing in different directions, that is usually the beginning of the end.

Like every man I have ever met, I put my own selfishness above my relationship. I had a wounded child's sense of entitlement to do as I pleased and as destructively as possible. After all those years as a professional musician and pot addict, I believed I needed marijuana to be creative. Even worse, in 1979 I started using cocaine to join the music business in-crowd, but the drug immediately started using me instead.

In 1979, Amy gave up. No, not on me, though no sane person would have blamed her if she had. She gave up using marijuana, which she had also been using daily, and cocaine, which she used in smaller doses than I had. I did not go along with her, or, to be more accurate, I did not *grow* along with her.

Amy's first panic attack had forced her to change her life, a classic example of how something terrible can help you to grow. She dedicated herself to conquering her panic attacks and informed me that she would no longer join me in the self-destructive aspects of the musician's life.

Even in the darkest days of my addiction, I was always in love with her, so I accepted her decision and also tried to support her fight against her panic attacks. Congratulating myself for being so supportive, I could not understand why she was being so aggressive about getting me to quit using. I was so drugged that I could not see that I was sick, let alone notice that my problem was a thousand times worse than hers and could not help but make her panic attacks worse. How could she count on a drug addict for anything, even one who was otherwise loving and affectionate? I am sure that her worries about me and my self-destructive behavior contributed to her anxiety problems.

I felt sorry for myself, one of the biggest mistakes anyone can make. This caused the beginning of a rift between us. I had "triangulated" our relationship, as our dear friend Dr. Gerry Epstein puts it in his book, *Healing Visualizations*. I was so addicted to cocaine and the lifestyle it thrives in that I was not only oblivious to the pain and suffering I was causing, I was afraid to stop, though I had not admitted that to myself yet.

Near the end of my period of addiction, I learned that my parents had a lot of secrets of their own, secrets that they had hidden from each other and their two children during the twelve years they were married. There was suicide and alcohol and drug abuse in their families. I was glad to finally hear the truth. While I was freely floating in my mother's amniotic fluid, she was desperately trying to keep the lid on her terrible secrets. I was literally steeping in a sea of anxiety. For the first ten years of my life, she kept her secrets from my father and he kept his from her. Even now, I often feel like I am keeping a dark secret. I used to suspect that I was keeping something from myself, but now I know that it is a feeling, not a fact.

I think that both of my suicidal grandparents were calling out to me, trying to get me to stop my own self-destructive behavior. I have no other explanation as to why, after all of those years, both my mother and father finally leveled with me. It was quite a shock, but in my drugged state, it registered as just another weird thing in my weird life.

Even knowing all of these things did not convince me to stop, not right away. That is the way addiction is. The revelations got my attention, but I actually felt cool and slightly validated, as if to say that drugs and depression ran in my family, so of course I was depressed and using drugs. Tradition! Still, along with the tendency toward depressive, addictive behavior, I also inherited my intelligence and my good health from my grandparents, so I totally forgive them and thank them profusely. Two out of three isn't bad!

Astrology teaches us that everyone is unique, and it is easy to see that this is true. Drugs and other healing modalities that cure some people kill others. Although Alcoholics Anonymous and other programs counsel against continual confrontation with an addict, Amy did exactly that, and I am glad and drug-free for it. She fought me every day and, though I hated what she was doing, I loved her and put up with it. I did not even realize that she was feeling the exact same way about me!

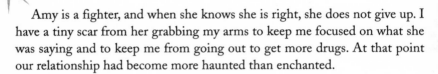

Amy is a fighter, and when she knows she is right, she does not give up. I have a tiny scar from her grabbing my arms to keep me focused on what she was saying and to keep me from going out to get more drugs. At that point our relationship had become more haunted than enchanted.

> **Secret: Unconditional love helps you be more understanding.** Your lover is your best friend—you must be there for each other in every way. You must feel you can trust one another completely and can turn to each other for support and gentle guidance when one of you feels weak. Remember, a maternal nature exists in us all.

We married in 1978, when Amy and I were twenty-seven and twenty-eight, respectively, during the time of what astrologers call our Saturn "transit." This has nothing to do with buses, trains, or subways, but everything to do with how you are moving in your life.

The planet Saturn takes approximately twenty-eight years to go around the solar system, and your first Saturn transit marks your passage from youth to adulthood. Some people accept this passage and begin to act like adults, but others, even people like me who know astrology and should have known better, try to keep going along like overgrown kids. Saturn doesn't like that and tells you so. Your life starts to seem like you are moving slowly, as if you were suspended in a gelatinous sticky slime. My music "career" was going nowhere.

When Saturn "speaks," you had better listen, but I did not. Saturn rules discipline, time, and structure, among other things, including the structure of our bodies—our bones. I had broken my wrist clowning around like the undisciplined stoned idiot that I was, the same wrist from which I had lost a solid gold ID bracelet given to me by Amy's mother, the chain of which had belonged to Amy's father, Ray. To make things worse, I had gone to a very old doctor whose equally old X-ray equipment missed detecting the break in my wrist. Instead, he told me that I had sprained it and that it would hurt for a while, which it did, especially when I did push-ups on my knuckles, a karate exercise. The pain got so intense that I mentioned it to my friend Jay Polikoff's father, the late great violinist Max Polikoff, who was a fan of my music. His concern for his valuable hands was so great that he would not open a jar. He gave me the name of Hand Surgery Associates and when I went to them, Dr. Malone's state-of-the-art X-ray found the break in my scaffoid bone and the necrosis that had set in from six months without treatment. He ordered me into the hospital the next day for microsurgery and, since we could not afford to pay for his miraculous, pioneering operation, he offered to let me pay on time if I promised not to sue the old doctor who had misdiagnosed me.

This tangled event was only one of the many worries for my beloved Amy as, after failing to come home again the previous night, I drove across midtown Manhattan to my sister's apartment where we were then staying for extended periods of time. I had done yet another all-nighter, this time with the guitarists of two of the world's most famous bands, and I was feeling my non-famous status profoundly. These guys were such conspicuous consumers of drugs that they actually disgusted me and made me feel sorry for them as we said good-bye (talk about denial!).

I was also sad, clammy, anxious, and my heart was racing—classic symptoms of withdrawal. I felt like the Energizer Bunny must feel on those rare occasions when he is just about to quit going and going and going. Emotionally, I was a total wreck, but I had convinced myself that I was a good enough driver to concentrate totally on the mechanics of driving to keep my car from becoming a total wreck, too. I valued my life and my love, unlike most of the unfortunate fellow addicts I had met.

However, even my carefully controlled facade crumbled when I ran into the most horrendous morning traffic jam I had ever seen. As luck would have it, I was stopped by a white-gloved policeman at the corner of 57th Street and Broadway, and then found myself in a sea of policemen. Thanks to my youth, this made me feel secure rather than threatened. Just then, a fifty-foot-tall balloon of Bullwinkle the Moose floated by and I realized that I was watching and had almost become part of the Macy's Thanksgiving Day Parade. Something about the absurdity of it all hit me hard.

Amy did not confront me when I got home. She just cried and cried from the deepest place within her, her wrenching sobs shaking me to my core. She sounded like a wounded animal. I had never heard anything like it and hope I never do again. When I awoke that afternoon, she was gone and I found a note from her informing me that things had gotten so bad that I was losing her. Like a real addict, this news caused me to reach for my false life preserver, the little plastic grinder that I used to powder up rocks of cocaine so that I could snort it.

As I turned the handle on top of it around and around with my right hand, which was in a cast from my knuckles to my biceps, the absurdity of that desperate scene and the hell that I had made our lives into finally hit me. I was a cocaine addict! I was a cliché! I was going to lose Amy, my Soul Mate, because I had been too weak and stupid to see what was really going on. I had made the lives of the people I loved miserable and put them in danger. And those were just the first things I realized and regretted; the list is endless.

Though I am told these kinds of realizations are more likely to make an addict feel even more sorry for himself and therefore more self-indulgent, my love for Amy saved the day. When it came down to it, I loved her more than cocaine, no contest there. I threw away all my drugs, drug paraphernalia, and my drug friends before I threw away my life; not everyone is so fortunate.

Amy and I did not care what else happened—we could live in our house or the poor house—as long as I stopped doing drugs, which I did. I ate roast beef and chocolate for breakfast for a couple of weeks. I needed that kind of jolt to replace the ones I had given up.

I am proud of the fact that after we went through our years of troubles, I was brave enough to finally realize that she was right and, like her, do the hard work of detoxifying and redefining myself. Amy's unorthodox method to stop smoking cigarettes when she first met me had been to roll up about an ounce of marijuana and smoke the joints like cigarettes, until she got completely sick of it. I am sure that technique would *not* have worked for me. Being an extreme Aquarian, I had to go from being completely addicted to stopping cold turkey.

Acupuncture restored my balance, and we both have sought regular treatment from other Oriental medicines for the past twenty years. Both kinds of care have helped us tremendously. By combining them with natural foods and vitamins, the Bach flower remedies (a miraculous system of thirty-eight flower essences, each with its own unique healing effect on a specific mental attitude), breath awareness, and most of all, by giving ourselves and each other comfort, support, and acceptance, we survived our dark night of the soul, which taught us important lessons that we now offer you as a cautionary tale. If you are in the grip of something more powerful than you are, get help. It may be considered orthodox or unconventional, but if it helps you remember your spirit and return to your center, that's what you should be doing.

Amy and I both know the truth: just as she is always vulnerable to panic attacks, I will always be an addict. The only thing that works on addicts is to replace your addiction with a more positive addiction. For instance, become addicted to seeing how you feel without drugs.

I did not plunge right in on making a living, even though things were very difficult for us for a time. I took the slow but steady approach. I had one job and that was to avoid backsliding. I am proud to say that I never relapsed. Since I stopped, on the three or four occasions where I dreamed I was taking drugs, I was horrified to see myself do so, even in a dream, and I would awake frightened as if from a nightmare. I really do enjoy being clear-headed. I feel so sorry for those who have added substance abuse to the list of life's challenges we all have.

I replaced my drug addiction with a dedication to rebuilding my life and to making amends—with Amy, her mother, and my sister. I'm also making up for lost time. My family, or at least the only part of my family who knew I even used drugs (until now!) was very loving and forgiving. The hardest part was making amends with myself. It was all worth it.

> **Secret: Forgiveness is an antidote to pain.** All too often the tendency is not to try to solve the problem but to fix the blame. It is not a weakness but the greatest strength to forgive. Especially, forgive yourself. Accept your human frailty as a natural part of your being, and your mistakes as signs of your efforts to grow.

Amy: The Lords of Overload Meet Chronic Fatigue

Like everyone, we have been through several major dark nights of the soul. We have experienced crisis, defeat, sickness, and challenges that tested our belief in ourselves or in the healers or practitioners who tried to help us. We've even doubted our intuition, for all the guidance it had given us. I do believe nevertheless that we wouldn't appreciate all the love, light, and laughter that multiplied and grew in geometric progression with the healing of our wounds were it not for our difficulties.

We now know that the heart grows bigger with compassion when we share the connection that thankfulness, reverence, and humility inspire. These experiences are the shadows that shape our lives and transform us into spiritual, metaphysical beings, for the shadow forces the light to come from deep within us, the profoundly self-realized reunion with what is our true eternal essence.

By 1993, Monte and I had completed four book and card sets: *Karma Cards, The Enchanted Tarot, The Alchemist, Goddess Guide Me*, and our fifth one, *The Psychic Circle*, was about to be released. We had created and sold our first two book and card deck divination systems, *Karma Cards: A New Age Guide to Your Future Through Astrology*, which Penguin Books published in 1988, and *The Enchanted Tarot*, which St. Martin's Press published in 1990, with the help of one of Britain's finest and most successful book packagers, Eddison/Sadd Editions, Ltd. However, by the time we were working on *The Enchanted Tarot*, we were already so confident about the way it could and should be done that the British book packagers kept saying, "What do you need us for?" And so for our next project, *The Alchemist: The Formula for Turning Your Life to Gold,* we decided to become book packagers ourselves, not really knowing how we were going to do it, but going ahead and getting the deal anyway. Thankfully, our now dear friend, the legendary St. Martin's Press editor, Thomas Dunne, saw in us the spark of something that gave him the confidence to let us do it on our own, for which we will be eternally grateful. Being book packagers meant that we not only had to invent, write, and illustrate our creations, we had to design, manufacture, and deliver finished books to our publishers for them to promote and distribute. Plus, because we acted as our own agent and lawyer, and took a very hands-on approach to the marketing and advertising of our work, we had more work than we had ever dreamed of. Being a book packager is stressful enough; learning how to be one is twice as stressful. Were it not for my having the expert sewing assistance of my high school friend Mary Jane Seely I could not have done it.

Besides being the creative director of our new book packaging enterprise, I had created four hundred tapestries and collages, 138 of which were designed to illustrate our four book projects. At the same time, I was finishing up my third children's book with my mother, entitled *The Dream Quilt.* On top of it all, Monte and I were attending trade shows and conventions to promote these titles and also traveling to do book-signings and radio and TV appearances.

In the midst of this full-tilt creative blitz, we met Richard and Randye Worth, who owned Frookies, a fruit-sweetened cookie company. We were at a brunch with Dan Rattiner, the gifted writer and founding publisher of *Dan's Papers,* the most widely read newspaper on the North and South forks of Eastern Long Island, New York. The South Fork contains the Hamptons where we reside in the same house my family and I moved to from Laporte, Pennsylvania, in 1967.

As we often do, we were reading our tarot cards for Susyn Reeve, who was then Dan's wife, and for his other guests. Richard was amazed with our inventiveness. We liked him right away! He said, "Think of a cookie idea, and lets see what we can do together."

Of course, the next morning Monte and I woke up, looked at each other, and said, "Fortune Frookies—the game you love to eat." He loved it! The design, promotion, and attention of this new project folded into all the other things we had to do.

There's a saying that goes something like, "The more you have to do, the more you get done." It's true, but it's also true that the more broken out your skin is, the more it will stay that way until you give it a break. It's also true that the bigger the bags under your eyes, the puffier they will become if you don't get some rest. And finally it's also true that the more tired you are, the more tired you will get if you keep pushing yourself. I was about to learn all of these lessons.

I think all of this started to dawn on me when I developed a terrible headache for three months straight (while I went to the Frankfort Book Fair to promote a new book and went on a book tour to demonstrate our psychic talking board—a stressful feat in itself). Did I mention that my ninety-five-year-old grandmother had moved in to live with us and my mother?

To make a long story short, I developed a flu that seemed to last for two months, plaguing me with a constant sore throat and swollen glands. My local doctor prescribed antibiotics. I got sicker. While I was sick, I still socialized, because, hey, I didn't really have time to be sick—I had a lot to do, places to go, people to see!

At another exhausting dinner party, we met a wonderful couple, Dr. Robert M. Giller and his beautiful wife, Nancy Lee. They seemed very much in love and we liked being around them and that energy. As we chatted that evening, we discovered that Bob, Dr. Bob as we came to call him, was quite a well-known natural doctor and one of the first acupuncturists to practice in the States in the early 1970s. We became fast friends.

I didn't even mention my illness, as I think I was still in denial. I had been taking vitamins and going for acupuncture for years, which helped me with my anxiety, but not with my A-type personality. That would take more than needles. I apparently needed to be laid low for a while in order to go to my next level. In retrospect, I realize that at that time I was using these modalities to fuel me for more work, to get more done. I didn't have time to waste. I was completely driven, partly to prove something to myself, and partly out of a survival instinct—being a freelance artist will do that to you.

At one point, Monte and I found ourselves dressed like a warlock and a witch, standing in the aisle of a food trade-show, promoting our Fortune Frookies. We are professionals and always do what is required of us. Monte likes to say that we only have two speeds, off and on. However, I was still making and selling my art, and the goofiness of our cookie-promotion act clashed mightily with my sense of myself as a serious artist.

I remember a group of very coarse food-industry men in suits walking by, smoking, and asking me, "Are you a good witch or a bad witch?" At the tenth time I heard those words that day, I was becoming a very bad witch. All the recent stressors of my grandmother, meeting deadlines, art career frustrations, and spreading myself too thin added up badly. Where had all my power gone? Where had all my immunity gone?

In the following weeks, Dr. Bob observed my symptoms and invited me to his office for some tests. When the tests came back, he said it was just as he thought: I had elevated Epstein-Barr virus titers, strong indicators for Chronic Fatigue Syndrome. It has many symptoms, many labels, and many victims. He explained that with intravenous vitamin injections and specific acupuncture to restore balance in my body, a diet higher in protein, and less stress, I would get better. I trusted him because he had had this condition himself, some years earlier. He assured me that I would get better, but it would take time. I was lucky to have such a knowledgeable and understanding doctor who was also my friend.

I was also lucky to have such a wonderful and supportive husband. My case was probably exceptional because many people go misdiagnosed with this illness and are misunderstood to the point of questioning their own sanity. At the time, most doctors did not believe that there was any such disorder caused by the Epstein-Barr virus and dismissed the symptoms as psychosomatic.

It is a disease that can certainly put a strain on relationships, but Monte was the prince of a man that makes him so unique. He made me feel safe and loved even in my most helpless state. There were months where I felt so sick that merely taking a shower was a day's work! I would describe it as feeling like a limp dishrag, day after day.

Once a week, Monte would help me to our car and drive me to New York City to get my special vitamin injection. That was a two-and-a-half-hour trip each way. He would pull the car up to the doctor's office, wait outside with the motor running while I got the treatment, and whisk me home again. I'm sure I was a depressing bore, but Monte was always cheerful for me, rooting for me, loving me. It truly deepened our love, because these terribly difficult situations make you see and appreciate the heroic side of your Soul Mate that you might not otherwise see. And your love deepens.

I saw that Monte loved me even when I wasn't making art every minute—that's how much I defined myself through my accomplishments. When I was ill, I felt guilty that I couldn't keep up my normal pace. I blamed myself for being sick with such a mysterious illness. I felt ashamed for not having the energy to deal with other people's problems; for feeling cranky, for feeling vulnerable. I felt terrible. But Monte always made me feel like a whole person. And that gave me a lot of hope.

Secret: **Trust the process.** Have faith that there is a divine plan. Worry only creates stress and accomplishes nothing. If you realize that most difficulties you encounter are for the best in the long run, you manifest the positive attitude that can bring wonderful relationships to you. All you have to do is follow your heart, take small steps forward on your path, and trust. Let the future wait and take care of itself. Take time to be in the moment and experience life with a gentle purity.

Taking care of myself became a priority. Adjusting some of my attitudes was a big part of that. I also let myself be helped by some wonderful healers. My main healer was Monte: he knew I was sick because he knows me so well. He convinced me that I would recover. He did not dismiss my complaints, and he helped me adjust to being weak and slowed down. That kind of empathy and compassion disables even your worst self-criticism and shows you how to be kinder to yourself. Letting yourself be helped is crucial to recovery. It is always a great comfort that other people care. You have to seek out the truly sympathetic help, though. Most people lack a full understanding unless they've had a similar personal experience.

Chronic Fatigue Syndrome is a very strange and isolating illness. It takes a lot of energy and time just to come to terms with it. Chronic Fatigue is actually a misnomer, because it suggests that you feel tired all the time. In actuality, you feel ill all the time. Getting enough sleep doesn't help—you still wake up feeling unrefreshed and fluish. Exercise made me feel more exhausted and more achy. I was very sensitive to changing barometric pressures. I felt rotten all the time. I wanted to feel normal again, to go out again, and to do more things, but since I felt like crap and couldn't, I felt "left out" of life. Friends who didn't understand the illness took it personally when I couldn't go out. People who are chronically ill want to remain capable and nurturing and feel badly if they are not doing their fair share. They also don't want to bore others with it, but they can't help getting hypersensitive if friends ignore their suffering. Above all, however, it's important to believe that you will get well.

And little by little, I did. I guess the whole process took about four years. At first, the acupuncture and the shots I would get in New York City would make me feel better for a few days, but by the end of the week their benefit wore off. But gradually, their effect would last longer. The recovery process is very much "two steps forward, one step back." You have good days and bad days. When you have a string of good days, you fool yourself into thinking that the end of the illness is near. A bad day can open up an abyss of hopelessness. When you feel well enough to do more, you will probably overdo it to make up for lost time, but you'll pay the price and feel sicker afterward. I read whatever I could on the subject, but some literature was scary, even suggesting that one might never recover.

There were many things and several people that I believe contributed to my recovery. Dr. Bob's protocol and advice were exactly right, and his friendship changed my life. My dear friend Dr. Epstein gave me some specific visualizations that took me to another level of improvement. My chiropractor, Dr. Fred Soroka, always gave me great advice and encouragement, and appropriate adjustments.

I received regular massages and changed my diet. I monitored my stress, and learned to say no. I prayed. I ate organic food. I detoxified. I cut out milk, wheat, and sugar. I took magnesium, L-5-Hydroxytryptophan, vitamin B-complex, lots of vitamin C, and antioxidants. I eliminated carbonated beverages. There is no single cause of this illness. For me it was a series of difficult life events at once that triggered it. But don't blame or criticize yourself for allowing illness into your life. Your healing can be a real turning point in your life, because you'll discover that you are the healer. And we all need to be healers.

> **Secret: Z-Z-Z—Get enough rest and take care of your stress.** Listen to your dreams. Practice calm. Slow down your breathing. Manage your time. Know your stress triggers. Laugh as much as possible. Get massages. Explore healing practices designed to cure problems on physical, mental, and spiritual levels. You must heal yourself before you can help others to heal.

Thanks to Monte and my mother, I never stopped making art or doing business during my illness. But now I am not so preoccupied with my career. Inside my head, I stopped driving myself so hard. I let go. I didn't put the same demands on myself, because doing so literally made me sick.

Although I have recovered, my illness will always mark a major transformative and defining experience of my identity. I am so lucky, and I am grateful for the ultimate freedom that this long-term illness gave me. It made a healer out of me so I could care for my mother during her difficult illness.

MONTE: REMEMBERING THAT TIME

Remembering Amy's illness is very emotional for me. Amy was very sick, but so was her mother, Jessie. Amy's grandmother Rena was a delicate old woman with her own health problems, and there we all were, living under one roof! Now I look back on it as the good old days. Though I'm physically strong and healthy, my emotional intelligence isn't always as sharp. However, I'm very good in a crisis, and there was no shortage of them then and now. I am proud that I rose to the occasion. Amy's praise in the foregoing paragraphs is the only medal of honor this man needs to feel like a true warrior.

The funny thing is that, with the major exceptions being the times when we needed to help Jessie and Rena, Amy and I are busier than ever now. However, we now know that you have to make your life into something that you can handle without making yourself sick. This takes absolute honesty with yourself, each other, and with the many people who want something from you, even if it is just to go out to dinner.

Amy and I long ago realized that we have control freak and perfectionist tendencies that we must always monitor. I came late to realizing I was a perfectionist because I figured that I couldn't be a perfectionist, since I wasn't very perfect!

Secret: **Working toward goals together is the essence of a living, breathing partnership.** Give support as needed. Concentrate and focus your energy on positive goals: health, fitness, creativity, spiritual growth. When you share love, you can enjoy knowing that you are helping your partner to live to the fullest. This is the secret of true joy and happiness in a committed relationship. Our relationship is as successful as it is because we have both decided it is the most important thing in our lives.

CHAPTER EIGHT

How to Meet Your Soul Mate: Accept No Substitutes

Meeting your Soul Mate is one of the most worthwhile things you can do. We wake up every morning knowing that we are two of the luckiest people in the world to be so in love. Everything we learn about life reinforces that knowing. If you have not yet experienced such a connection, you have something wonderful to look forward to.

The media is filled with stories of the most famous, accomplished, beautiful, rich, and powerful people who seem to have it all, yet who can't fully enjoy their success because they lack a Soul Mate to share it with. But believe us—if you put your efforts into becoming yourself fully and do your best to realize your potential and find out who you are and what you are capable of, you will become the kind of person your Soul Mate will want to meet and stay with.

Secret: Soul Mates work on their relationships by working on themselves. You know you have found your Soul Mate when you enjoy just watching your partner live, and you desire to make your partnership work and to be there for each other in every way.

The How to Grow a Soul Mate Checklist

When we last dated, back in 1974, the most hip, cool, and attractive thing you could be was yourself and as far as we are concerned, that hasn't changed. It is a logical way to go about meeting your Soul Mate. If you are yourself, then only people attracted to the real you will present themselves for your consideration. However, it is easy to see that if you are one of the above-mentioned famous, accomplished, beautiful, rich, and powerful people, or even a lesser version of them, you might attract people to you who are after other things besides the real you.

What advice can we offer that works for everyone, even those who are not only blessed with the gifts of this world but are also besieged by suitors after you for all of the wrong reasons? First, make sure that you reread the "How *Not* to Find Your Soul Mate Checklist" in chapter 6. In fact, some of you celebrities, the ones who believe your own press, had better commit it to memory!

Now, as to meeting a potential Soul Mate. It's not about where you go—charity functions, bars, the Internet. In other words, it's not about what you do, it's about how you do it, how you act, the kind of energy you send out. Where you go to meet people is irrelevant. Taking this book's advice "magnetizes" the right person to you. Use these checklists—and the whole book—to discern who you do and don't want. Begin to act accordingly, and see what happens.

Secondly, after you are certain that you or your potential partner are not manifesting any of those odious behaviors, try manifesting all of these:

1. ❑ Never take each other for granted. Show how lucky you feel to know each other and make sure to spend as much time together as possible. Work together, if you can. Giving little gifts for no special reason will delight your partner *and* yourself!

2. ❑ Treat each other as equals. You may not have the same background, looks, talents, connections, power, or potential, but you are two halves of the same team. Act like it.

3. ❑ Always compliment each other on good qualities and do it several times a day. If you like the way he/she looks, smells, or makes you feel today, say so.

4. ❑ Have concern for each other's total welfare, even if it causes you to reverse yourself on some long-cherished notion. Make the other person's needs as important as your own. Once you have determined that you have found your Soul Mate, you can make his/her needs more important than your own. Don't worry—you will want to do so.

5. ❑ Be kind. Really listen to each other's words, and try to understand each other's position. Do not assume that you know how the other feels. Ask when you want to know something. Never refuse to communicate.

6. ❑ Get to the root of anger, frustration, anxiety, and fear. Learn to tell when you are the problem and when you might be the solution, and try to be the solution more often than the problem.

7. ❑ Always show how happy you are to see each other and smile, even if you are in the middle of hearing the most annoying news. Remember, you are each the most important and powerful thing in each other's lives. Everything else is secondary.

8. ❑ Forgive each other and mean it. Have the courage to be imperfect. Admit it when you are wrong. Assume that you could be wrong, even when you think you are right; it is not as hard as it sounds.

9. ❑ Always use criticism carefully and constructively. Do not demand change from anyone but yourself. *Do not demand change from anyone but yourself.* It's important enough to say twice.

10. ❑ Share and explore your fantasies, dreams for the future, and the dreams you awaken from. Never go to sleep angry. Making up can do wonders for your ability to sleep soundly.

11. ❑ Compromise whenever possible, especially on matters of taste. Eat the same food so your breaths will smell the same. If that is impossible, do not eat foods or wear scents, styles, and colors that offend your Soul Mate.

12. ❑ Keep a positive attitude and a sense of humor, especially about yourself. No matter what happens, if you two are together, relatively healthy, and your bills are paid, laugh at the other stuff.

If your potential partner resists these twelve rules for Soul Mate nurturing, or if she does not treat you with the same caring and kindness, you will have to tell her. Don't give up on her if she makes an effort to change after you gently and tactfully make her aware of your concerns.

However, if you can't discuss your concerns with him because you think you're unable, unwilling, or if you fear his reaction, you must face the fact that you may not have met your Soul Mate just yet. If you had, you would both find a way to work things out; Soul Mates always do.

> **Secret: Appreciate all the good things in life.** Show your love. Show you care. Passion and compassion are what make you attractive. If you would enjoy the passion of love, you must act first with passion. Men are willing to go through a lot to earn the appreciation of their true love, and women, as the keepers of the sacred flame of life, desire to be given the respect they deserve. If you demonstrate your mutual appreciation, true love will deepen and last a very long time.

How We Found Each Other

This is probably the most enchanted chapter of all. This chapter contains our personal myth. Our myth is not made up; we lived every word you are going to read. But we still consider it a myth nonetheless. We cannot look back on the events and forces that brought us together and enabled us to live such a wonderful life together without being awestruck at the majesty of life's divine plan. Some think that there is no divine plan. That is their myth and they are welcome to it. We have seen too much to doubt.

> **Secret: Express yourself creatively.** You need to be appreciated for who you really are, so speak and let others know. Communication begins with an effort to make yourself clearly understood. It is easy to let fear and preconceived notions stand in the way of true communication. Also, taking an interest in how others express themselves (known as listening!) leads to sharing, and sharing leads to caring. Creative self-expression is true spirituality.

Our Personal Myth

Like our dream world, the world of myths and fairy tales is real and quite important to our everyday life. If children do not grow up with fairy tales, they are much more likely to lack the ability to let themselves feel happy when they grow older. The content of the fairy tale is less important than the secrets it reveals that will affect us all of our lives. Traditional myths offer us guidance through our own life's journey, even if we only appreciate them as a made-up story. In a very real way, we not only have to explain the myth, we have to enact it as well. Our life's journey is really to find our own myth, for myths help us make sense of our life and the world around us.

Like we said, we have been living together since 1975, married since 1978. It would be presumptuous of us to think that we could understand what dating must be like today, when having sex can mean a death sentence and people are clothes, body, and status conscious to a self-defeating degree we would have thought impossible.

However, we know that you know what it is like to live today and to be trying to bring love into your life and time, just like we did. We also know that you are going to transcend the problems of your time and meet your Soul Mate, just like we did. When you have lived your own myth like we have, we will be standing in line to buy your book. Good luck! Here is ours and from both points of view, too.

AMY: HOW I MET MONTE

"Monte and I met at the filming of a porno movie." This is how we truthfully and gleefully answer that question, though we often think that we'd get a better reaction by saying that we first met in a dream. Since Monte and I judge people more by our intuition than by anything else, we not only see their arched eyebrows, we feel them either marveling at what an interesting way to meet, disgusted that they might be talking with the transmitters of sexual and other diseases, or groping for some kind of a label to pin on us based on someone else.

Living in midtown Manhattan 1974, I was coming into my own as an artist. I experimented with new materials and techniques, especially the multilayered bedspread I hand-painted for the original Broadway production of the play *Chicago*. I was lucky enough to have an encouraging mother and creative friends. We would all go to see the latest exhibits, movies, and musical performances. I was very, very busy. Even though I was working designing props for Tony Walton, the Tony- and Academy Award–winning set designer, I was also taking night courses in graphic design at the School of Visual Arts.

I had always known that art was my life. My father's death left my mother without the financial resources for my tuition at her alma mater, Pratt Institute, but I was actually glad to be out in the real world. I was eager to express myself in as many ways as I could.

Although I had a "sometime" boyfriend and would go out with other men on occasion, I was not looking for a permanent relationship or marriage. In fact, the thought never occurred to me. I was more interested in learning about life and figuring out how I could make a living as an artist. That's when it happens—when you're engaged fully with something else!

When single people who are looking for a partner ask us for advice, we always suggest that they just do work that they love and that will attract the person whom they're meant to meet. It creates an energy vortex when you "follow your bliss," as the late Joseph Campbell so aptly put it. When we met, Monte was devoting himself to his music and I was getting deeper and deeper into my art. We weren't "looking," we were doing. This can make a person very attractive. When you are working hard at what you love, you are vibrating at just the right frequency, the frequency of love. It is no wonder that so many people fall for each other when they are in the throes of passionate commitment to a cause.

When my friend Sharon and I got together, we would sometimes go to parties. Though she was kind of ditsy and had some serious personal problems, she was fun. She would often mention her friend Monte, the man she

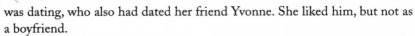

was dating, who also had dated her friend Yvonne. She liked him, but not as a boyfriend.

For a reason unknown to me at the time, every time she mentioned his name, a bell would go off in my head. I wondered why? That had never happened to me.

When I finally met Monte on that October day on the rooftop apartment on 22nd Street and Ninth Avenue, we were immediately attracted. It impressed me that he was so friendly and outgoing and that he was confident enough to play in that unusual setting of musicians, film crew, extras, and porn stars. As we gazed over the rooftops of New York City, he made me laugh by describing himself as a "mugician," a combination musician and magician. He impressed me by coining the word on the spot to explain his main interests, music and the search to understand the nature of personal reality. His enjoyment of life was infectious.

He was so big and strong, those intuitive eyes taking me in. Still, I didn't know he was "The One" until he chased me to walk me home after the concert and kissed me until I got chills. When he got close to me and massaged me deeply, just to make me feel better, I started to feel safe and warm in a way I had never felt before. We just continued to get warm together. In fact, we got hot, and we've stayed hot all these years.

MONTE: HOW I MET AMY

Like everything else about us, the way Amy and I met requires a little explaining and a lot of open mind. Amy's intense beauty and perennially purple hair; my one-button-over-the-line opened shirt collars shamelessly revealing my graying chest hairs, and irreverent sense of humor; Amy's refreshingly down-to-earth humility despite her artistic genius; my Aquarian delight in tweaking words and conventions, not to mention my lapsing into astrology-speak and expecting others to understand my explanations or at least try to—all these things and more conspire to make us, our art, and our creative output a lot more than what meets the eye upon first meeting us.

In our own first meeting, I was the one being paid to be in the porno movie. Amy was there as a guest and an extra. It was October of 1974, and this was supposedly the first feminist porno movie. Its working title was *Up the Girls*, a double entendre if ever there was one.

I was only appearing in the porno movie because I was a musician in a band hired to play for a rooftop party scene. It was a "clean" scene. I'm sorry if I disappoint, but all I did was play a fretless clear Lucite Dan Armstrong electric bass guitar. I was having a great time that day.

The band consisted of me, a woman who played the grand piano in an evening gown, and, that day, a veritable rebel army of Latin percussionists who represented almost all of the different nationalities of our neighbors south of the border. We usually had only five percussionists playing with us but the promise of a porno gig, even one where there was probably going to be no sex scenes filmed, brought out the noblest volunteer instincts in at least one each of our percussionists' friends and relatives. That day, we had a whole section of people who did nothing more than crane their necks and look around anxiously hoping to see something sexy as they banged sticks called claves together and shook maracas, not all together on the beat, either.

One of our regular drummers had built his own drums from crates of pigs' feet—you could still see the product name stenciled on the wood inside it. It was easy to see inside his drums because he had built a 60-watt lightbulb into them to keep his goatskin drumheads at the temperature of his native Brazil. These guys were the real McCoy, and we could play all day and night and often did. We never rehearsed because our music was totally improvised. However, that day, music was the last thing on my mind.

I remember seeing Amy for the first time. She walked out onto the penthouse's rooftop patio with my then-girlfriend Sharon, who was as tired of me as I was of her. My eyes immediately went to Amy, the most beautiful woman that I had ever seen. I gave Sharon a perfunctory hello kiss and then walked transfixed past her to Amy and asked her if she wanted a joint. This was a fairly standard part of the late 1960s teenage courtship ritual, which I'd not outgrown. Nor had I outgrown smoking pot, either. That would come years later.

We are often asked if we each knew we had found our Soul Mate the first time we met. Since the answer is "no," here is another secret.

> **Secret: Intuition is your inner vision—let it guide you.** Become aware, pay attention, listen—develop a psychic sense of your and your partner's true feelings. Validate each other's intuition. By observing our reactions to the messages offered to us by our intuition, we come to better understand our desires, our goals, and their motivations. We come to see what blocks us, what releases us out of our false selves, and what helps us to meet the challenge of our personal vision and myth.

As two people who have made their mark helping people to divine their future, we believe that it is crucially important to have great respect for your intuition and your ability to tap in to the divine within you and all things,

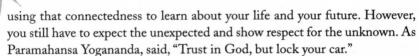

using that connectedness to learn about your life and your future. However, you still have to expect the unexpected and show respect for the unknown. As Paramahansa Yogananda, said, "Trust in God, but lock your car."

I sincerely believe my deepening commitment to my spiritual path and the respect that it taught me for the vastness of my spirit, my divinity, and especially the vastness of my ignorance saved me from having the kind of knee-jerk prejudices that, by all rights, might have prevented me from seeing Amy clearly.

By the time I met Amy, I'd read a lot of work by Jane Roberts, who produced several books, or at least she claimed they came through her, from a disembodied entity named Seth. These books, especially *The Nature of Personal Reality,* were beginning to "open the rusty gate," as martial artists refer to the painful stretching of their lower back and inner thighs in preparation for their strenuous kicking workouts. Only what was being stretched was my understanding of how my creaky beliefs affected my experience of reality.

Just as musicians develop their own style by copying the work of their favorite players, I read these works and tried to live their words in my thoughts and actions as an experiment with my own reality. Like many people in my generation, my desire to "get high" was an undisciplined attempt to emulate the sacred traditions of the indigenous people who used mind-altering substances as part of their religious practice for contacting their Higher Self.

In wanting to learn more, I hoped to find contentment. I was living the musician's life but my inner world was filled primarily with sorrow, confused yearnings, and loneliness. However, all that changed when I met Amy. As the Hindu sages wrote, "When the student is ready, the teacher appears." My teacher was Amy.

Prior to meeting Amy, I had been a strict vegetarian and, unfortunately, the kind of person you never want anywhere near you when you are eating or even thinking about eating. I was so boring. I did not eat any meat, fish, eggs, or dairy products, which is all well and good, but I was too likely to point out the errors in the eating habits of other people. I was filled with self-righteousness instead of love. The hypocrisy of purifying my body and then polluting it with drugs wasn't apparent to me then. Plus, I would fast for days at a time, sometimes a week or more. I liked doing that and might even do it again sometime, but it also had the effect of making me an even bigger pain in the butt than normal, lightheaded, and thin.

Thin as I was, I still had the self-image of my fat childhood years. I never thought of myself as skinny until I looked at a picture of myself years later taken when I was such a poor musician that I was living on peanut butter-and-jelly sandwiches and having to steal the jelly. That was the end of my homeless or "on the road" period. I was literally "on the skids," as they said in the Great Depression. I was spending my nights in a sleeping bag on wooden shipping pallets (skids) in a printing factory on 16th Street near Union Square owned by the father of my band's "manager."

I finally came to my senses and got so tired of being destitute that I stared at one spot on the wall and chanted "Nam Myoho, Renge Kyo" for hours. I had no idea what it meant, but I had heard that chanting these sacred words could bring you anything your heart desired. I later learned that the words are Japanese: *nam* = devotion, *myoho* = mystic law, *renge* = the law of cause and effect, and *kyo* = the teaching of the Buddha. Rather than doing this as some kind of cosmic wish list, many serious Buddhists consider repeating this chant to be the fundamental component of the practice of Buddhism and the phrase to express the ultimate truth of life and the universe.

I have to say that it worked. I got off my "too heavy for light work, too light for heavy work" artiste's ass and took the first job I could find, which was in the 47th Street jewelry district polishing rings until they and my fingernails shone like glass. I also began to be independent of my band, which was breaking up, much to my dismay. Our guitarist's girlfriend had inherited forty thousand dollars from her former boyfriend, a cop who had shot himself (over her leaving him, I think), and they were off to Tucson to open a macrobiotic health food restaurant. I was a rebellious musician trying to change the world and the way it judged me, my culture, and practically everything I believed in. What I did not see was how judgmental I was. I was not content just to believe in my vegetarian ways and let my good example be the best sermon. I thought that, compared to my guitarist and his girlfriend, I was not judgmental at all. Years later I learned firsthand living in the Hamptons and working on the movie *The Money Pit* that not one rich person thinks she's really that rich because she knows much richer people than herself. I was judgmental and I could not see it because I was not the most judgmental person I knew. My problem was not just about food. I had said several times that I would never go out with a woman who wore eye makeup! It is a good thing that I was able to see through my own prejudices and Amy's heavy eye makeup and into her rich brown eyes and her sweet heart. My spiritual training and the ability to remember that I might be wrong is what saved me from a life without true love.

There were early hints that I would find Amy. I later realized that in my years previous to meeting her, every time I heard the name "Amy," I did get a strange sensation. I am actually still friends with the first Amy in my life, Amy Krakow (formerly Ginsburg), and every time I heard her name called in the classroom from kindergarten through sixth grade, it did have a different feel to it from anyone else's name. My Amy later told me that when our mutual friend Sharon invited her to "come watch her friend Monte play music in a porno movie," a sort of bell went off in her head, too. However, we might never have gotten together had it not been for the circumstance of our second meeting.

A Patti Smith concert got our relationship into high gear, though Amy and I never heard a note of it. Sharon and I double-dated with Amy and one of the several weird guys she was dating at the time, and Dan Romer, who had been a fellow student with both women at Pratt Institute in Brooklyn, right down the street from where I was living. The concert was held at the then-dilapidated Roosevelt Hotel next to the then equally dilapidated Grand Central Station, both of which were only a few blocks from the seediest section of 42nd Street and Times Square and the theater that probably premiered *Up the Girls*, if it ever came out.

The concert was well attended, too well attended for Amy's claustrophobic date. Having grown and stretched myself from being a fat kid into a fit six feet, four inches tall, I can usually see over any crowd and so claustrophobia is not one of my problems. However, as we waited for them to open the doors of the ballroom, even I felt trapped by the crush of the growing crowd. Amy's date was not a musician, and his phobia was stronger than his desire to get what he paid for, but he still surprised all of us by bolting the concert, shouting how he couldn't take it any more, without one word of regret to Amy.

Amy's heavy eye makeup, wild hair, and costume—she was one of the first women of her time to wear her home-dyed purple overalls and men's work boots—gave her the appearance of a very tough New York cookie, but inside she was the sweet person I was about to fall in love with. She was offended by being so unceremoniously dumped, but she was not about to show anything but being pissed off and, after saying good night to us all, turned and headed out the door and out of my life.

We three survivors of this awkward episode discussed what had just happened and silently reviewed the new dynamic of our situation. Suddenly, in one of those life-changing moments, words started tumbling out of my mouth unbidden. I asked Dan if he would look after Sharon, he said sure, so I said good night to her, whom I never saw again. I cut a path like a football player running to daylight through the crowd of surprised concert-goers, who thought I was an undercover cop trying to arrest someone and tried to slow me down. I pushed through them like a man possessed, which I guess I was.

Once outside, I ran to the corner and saw Amy several blocks away steaming up a deserted Madison Avenue alone, even though it was late at night. Like I said, she was tough. I took off at top speed and when she heard my size thirteens clomping up the street behind her, she wheeled around ready to kill whoever was after her. She seemed quite surprised that it was me. I told her the truth as I knew it, that I did not want her to walk home alone, and she smiled that smile that I had seen the first day I met her, the smile that fuels my life now every day.

We walked together from 46th Street and Madison all the way to her home in the Coliseum Apartments, situated behind the now defunct New York Coliseum, a distance of several miles that seemed to go very quickly. It went so quickly that neither of us wanted our time together to end at her doorstep, and so we stopped to sit on one of the massive granite benches below the imposing statues at the Columbus Circle entrance to Central Park. Amy read my palm, which I found strange but interesting, and apparently liked what she saw, so we moved onward and upward to her room in the apartment she shared with her mother, who she said was a wonderful person and would not mind my spending the night with her. I liked her mother, Jessie, already.

I also liked everything about Amy's room, even though I could not see much because the only light was the regular New York City "moonlight," the light of the city bright enough to almost wash out a universe full of stars. There was compelling art on her walls, and I was intrigued to learn that not only was it original, either Amy or her friends at Pratt Institute had made it. We never had any real art that I can remember in my own house when I was growing up, yet for some reason I excelled at art above all my other school subjects. My aunt Rosie, who lived across the street from us, had a particular snow scene reproduction that I loved. I hoped that I would not say anything too stupid and reveal my cultural illiteracy.

We lay on Amy's bed, which was on the floor and had a gauzy curtain going all around it like something out of *The Thousand and One Nights*. There was a low, red wooden table that she had painted with the forms of white birds. And the smell! Amy wore a scent called "Wisteria" from Mary Quant, a name from the days when Carnaby Street in London was the center of the fashion world, and it drove me fairly crazy.

But what really made me fall in love with Amy was not just lying with her. It was the truth that came out of her mouth. That night and in the nights and

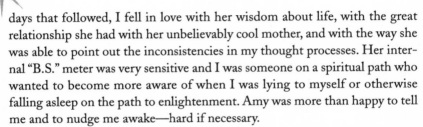

days that followed, I fell in love with her wisdom about life, with the great relationship she had with her unbelievably cool mother, and with the way she was able to point out the inconsistencies in my thought processes. Her internal "B.S." meter was very sensitive and I was someone on a spiritual path who wanted to become more aware of when I was lying to myself or otherwise falling asleep on the path to enlightenment. Amy was more than happy to tell me and to nudge me awake—hard if necessary.

I loved her laugh and she loved my sense of humor, though she tended to slap me in the face if I said something particularly funny, a habit I had to break her of later, since unless I am feeling down, I am always funny. She laughed at all of my jokes, and I loved that she thought I was funny, until I realized that she laughed at everything, seeing the humor in things that I thought imperfect. However, she did think I was smart, and her slaps served as true appreciation for a while, so I made do. She also coughed and sneezed every time she saw me, as if she was allergic to me. More likely she was allergic to the single-parent family of cats that lived with me after a former girlfriend dumped them on me as a good-bye present. Like many of our problems at that time, she overcame her allergy, and our lives have been enriched beyond compare by our first cat, Kit-Kat, our calico Muse without whom we wouldn't have been able to endure the loss of friends and family during the past few years, and now by Lacey Boots, another spirited little calico, and her brother, Zane Gray, a big, strong, and sweet tiger-striped adventurer, like his namesake.

I would be lying if I told you that my relationship with Amy progressed on a straight line toward our living together in May of 1975. More than a few times, it looked like we would not move closer than our fears and bad habits would allow. Amy, quite rightly, was wary of men, all men, and continued to go out with other people, and so did I. Though I did not like it when she dated several of the other musicians in one of the other bands I played in who, like me, were backing up Curtis Knight, the man who discovered Jimi Hendrix, I never said anything.

I held my tongue even when the violinist, a totally bald martial artist who also fancied himself a Zen master, started whacking Amy and even her mother with a Zen stick for not sitting correctly in their zazen meditation.

Striking someone across the shoulders while practicing zazen is a real part of Zen practice, called *kyosaku,* used especially during a zazen *sesshin,* the week-long meditation that is the capstone of committed Zen practice. In real practice, kyosaku has the effect of relieving tension in the shoulder muscles and focusing the mind away from physical discomfort. Moreover, Zen priests wait for the student to ask for the kyosaku. However, it was preposterous that this self-proclaimed "master" was getting his jollies pretending to be administering the blows for religious purposes.

However, I figured if they were crazy enough to take that, then they were not who I thought they were anyway. I realized that it was none of my business to tell anyone who she should go out with, even though all of these guys ran their mouths about her the way all too many guys do, and even when she, for some reason, talked to me about going out with them. It hurt, but I kept my mouth shut out of principle: Never let anyone see she is getting to you, especially if you think that's what she wants to see. Who wants to be with someone who does not want to be with you? Certainly not me or Amy and I hope not you. You cannot have an enchanted relationship if you have to force someone to be with you exclusively. In fact, we never asked each other to stop seeing other people. We just stopped.

> **Secret: Quest for truth.** When you have taken the time and done the work of establishing initial truthfulness and trust, you will find that it frees up an incredible amount of energy that can be used to accomplish many important things. Remember, you cannot be truthful with another person unless you are first truthful with yourself.

Chapter Nine

How We Got Engaged and Married

Bet you think you're going to read an elaborate hearts-and-flowers engagement story, don't you? Something like hiding a ring in a pogo stick. Or having "Marry Me!" spelled out in fireworks on the Fourth of July—high season where we live. Or asking a friend who directs the most popular talk show on TV to have one of us in the audience holding up a sign saying "Will you be mine?" while the other sat at home watching. Make no mistake. We're not opposed to grand gestures, romantic riffs, or displays that let the whole world know how much we love each other. In fact, we're in favor of them, and have been known to indulge in them from time to time. But our decision to marry wasn't like that.

The decision to get married is one of the most important decisions you will ever make, so if you do not read anything else in this book, read this chapter. If you still want to get married by the end of it, or if you are married and still want to stay married, then you will know that you are making the right decision. If you are with someone and this chapter makes you realize that you would be better living apart, then we will be just as happy. The point is that you have a right to be happy and to create your own enchanted world, either by yourself or with another person—maybe even with more than one, if that is your decision.

Remember how we have said before that to have an enchanted relationship, you have to put your relationship first? We are going to say it again here and we'll probably say it again later, too. It can't be stated too often. You have to put your relationship first, ahead of everything else in your life. Doing that will give you a great life together, even if you just pledge your troth to each other and skip getting married legally or having any kind of a public commitment ceremony. However, if you put your relationship first, one day you may

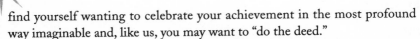

find yourself wanting to celebrate your achievement in the most profound way imaginable and, like us, you may want to "do the deed."

Here is a very powerful secret. Consider it our wedding gift to you: Do not get married to each other until you are already married to each other.

This marriage secret is similar to one of the most misunderstood secrets of that most misunderstood of esoteric practices, alchemy. One of the most basic alchemical principles is that "no alchemist can make gold until it is already in his possession."

Most people think of alchemy as the misguided quest by generations of medieval scientists to turn lead into gold. Alchemy was a system that sheltered not only chemistry but also philosophy from the vicious ignorance of the medieval Church and times. The "gold" that a real alchemist sought was a perfected soul expression, living life in tune with the highest principles imaginable. This "gold" was to be extracted from the "lead" of their unperfected soul by the study and practice of alchemy's teachings. Only a spiritually developed being already in possession of this "gold" could attain the wisdom and powers needed to make physical gold.

For the same reason that no alchemist could make gold unless they already possessed it, couples should not get married unless they are already married, because only a couple who is already so in love that they have no doubts about their desire to spend the rest of their lives together should get married. Until then, you might as well just live together, like we did from May of 1975 until June 11, 1978, until you realize that you cannot live without each other or that you cannot live with each other for another moment.

The Moment of Truth

For us, that moment of truth came when we discovered that Amy's maternal grandmother, Lilias ("Rena") Burtenshaw, was refusing to visit our home on the grounds that we were unmarried and "living in sin." We remember the day Jessie came up to our bedroom sadly explaining how she missed Rena and why she would not visit us.

So we said, "So, let's get married!"

Sorry to disappoint those who believe this has to be a moment created with infinite preparation. If you would like to make your engagement a big production, we are all for it, as long as you sustain your level of excitement and caring through to the marriage ceremony and then on through the rest of your life together. For too many people, romance comes in short, contrived bursts, rather than during a sustained lifetime of affection.

It was time. We had been living together for almost three years and for all intents and purposes, especially loving each other, we *were* married.

So we decided we might as well have the party and get the presents. That sounded easy enough. (And for those of you thinking that's true, read on.)

Some people think that marriage is an archaic form of bondage. They ask why should laws and government interfere with our right to pursue our happiness, though they are usually talking about the right to have sex with anyone they choose. If you are still looking for your Soul Mate, it's okay to have multiple sexual partners (as long as you practice safe sex, of course). But once you find her or him, there's every reason to settle into the relationship for life. The two of us have astrological charts that reveal such strong individuality that even the astrology novice might suggest we never marry anyone! Yet we found each other, and once we did, the idea of continuing to search never came into our heads.

By renewing your commitment to your Soul Mate, maybe with a party or marriage renewal (or wedding, if you've never been married), you can put some more enchantment in your relationship. But if you're questioning whether you're ready or whether he or she is the one, then remember the maxim: Don't get married until you're already married. By agreeing to get married, we gave each other the ultimate praise.

> **Secret: Love makes a sacred space in our lives where true growth and healing can happen.** When we love and are loved, we have someone with us we can trust to help and advise us, someone who has our best interests at heart. When you love someone, you want to be with him or her as much as possible, because committed happiness makes life seem very short indeed.

How We Got Married

One of the secrets to keep in mind if you decide to get married is that *getting* married is one of the hardest parts of *being* married. Put another way, it's almost impossible to throw a wedding without throwing a fit—or two or three. You'll make decisions based on your needs and beliefs, and you won't believe how those decisions affect others in your family.

Weddings are big business in this country. And you can plan a wedding to suit almost any taste and any budget. We think the most important thing to remember is that it's your wedding. Let it reflect the two of you and the couple you have already become. But first . . .

Some of the Hardest Parts

Money is at the top of the list. Deciding who to invite is a major test of your finances *and* your attitude about your finances.

It's incredible to us that people spend literally obscene amounts of money trying to impress people or to show their love in terms of dollars and loss of sense. There are so many silly conventions and outright superstitions that people cling to, not out of respect but out of fear of offending someone, or out of fear of originality, or to take the easy way out. Why not risk making an original statement of your own? When we do attend an original wedding, our hearts soar because we know that such a couple has a much better chance of making their marriage work. We're not against people spending their disposable income on a big celebration. We're simply saying it's important to make the ceremony your own.

When and where are important to your wedding and your relationship. Choose a date that works for you, according to your belief system or perhaps for the symbolism or memory. We've heard of people who got married on their parents' wedding anniversary, for instance. Be conscious of the date you're choosing and how it works for the two of you.

As astrologers, we picked the date for our wedding astrologically, not to ensure the success of our marriage, but to avoid the expense of renting a tent. We did not have much money. Had it not been for Jessie's allowing us to pay her a very low mortgage and only two-thirds of the bills, we might not have survived the financial pressures that destroy so many promising relationships and so many artists' careers, though we believe that we would have found another way.

Sure enough, the day dawned as one with the most perfect weather in memory. Unfortunately, June 11, 1978, happened to be the Jewish holiday Simchas Torah, the only day in the Jewish religion when you are absolutely prohibited from marrying.

Which leads directly to another of the really hard parts—who's on the guest list. Deciding who to invite is sort of like watching your life pass before your eyes. In our case, we invited some people that, in retrospect, maybe we shouldn't have.

MONTE: MY FAMILY

My father's side of the family was religious in a cover-your-ass-against-God's-wrath kind of way and had told him that they were not coming because marrying on Simchas Torah was a sin they wanted no part of. Amy and I didn't really care if they came, since we believe that if people do not want to be with you, then you do not need to be with them. My father must have pleaded with them because they put aside their fear of becoming collateral damage when the wrath of God befell Amy and me and deigned to come witness our nuptials.

Unfortunately for them, they also put aside their good manners. The wedding gifts they brought us must have been meant to show their disdain for our flaunting of the Holy Writ. Let's just say that their gifts were less than thoughtful, especially in the case of the used carving knife set and can opener that we received from our richest relatives.

Though it might not sound like it, it is the thought that counts with us. We have never been the kind of people who need things to be happy. However, the one thing that gets to us is to not feel supported, valued, and protected by those we feel close to, or who we are trying to feel close to. We always try to be thoughtful and considerate of everyone. When our relatives showed such a lack of both for us, especially on our wedding day, we felt bad for a time. Luckily, we have such a good life that we expect and even welcome a little rain now and then. Our relatives' indifference made us realize that we still had a ways to go in our quest not to let negative opinions of others affect us.

We've had practically nothing to do with any of them since that day. In truth, we have little in common, and from our point of view they're not interested in changing and growing. So the best thing to do is to bless them and wish them the best. Nothing says that you have to spend your time with people just because you are related to them. If this sounds unduly harsh, then prepare to have a less than enchanted relationship. Making your boundaries and deciding who you want in your life is crucial if you want to create your own enchanted world.

If you and your partner are a complete team, able to isolate yourselves from any negative influences, then you're on your way. If you do not draw close then, your marriage is off to a rocky start.

Deciding who sits next to whom is another test—a test of your ability to make mistakes or, put another way, not to expect perfection from yourselves. You simply cannot seat everyone perfectly. No matter what you do, somebody will complain about something, probably nothing you've even thought of. I experienced this when I worked in the movie business as a location manager, where part of my job was to throw a fast luncheon every day for seventy or more very well-paid, tired, and finicky people. You can have the best food in the world, but someone is going to complain about something. For your

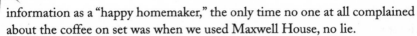

information as a "happy homemaker," the only time no one at all complained about the coffee on set was when we used Maxwell House, no lie.

The moral of that story is that it's not how expensive the food or coffee is. It's that you can't please all of the people all of the time. So, please, remember who's getting married. Remember, deciding to get married is a tribute you pay each other, a gift you give each other, not a debt you owe each other or your families.

How You Begin Is Likely to Be How You'll Go On

If you are not willing to stand up to friends and relatives who want more from you than you're willing to give, then we hope you have enough spare time for smoothing over the situations into which you will plunge yourself and your new marriage. However, if you're willing to see things as they are and make the tough choices that are necessary to make your base secure, you have a good chance of making this relationship last a lifetime. People who don't secure their base by putting their relationships first are probably doomed to wait until their second marriage to to get it right.

If you're worried about overpowering forces like troublesome relatives outside your marriage, you might want to consider making a prenuptial agreement. We never even thought of doing that, in part because we were quite poor at the time, and we certainly did not marry each other for our assets. But we must admit that we are prejudiced against prenuptial agreements. To us, a prenuptial is a prepackaged, freeze-dried divorce; it's always there for you to open up, add tears, and get a couple of lawyers to stir it up for you.

We are both almost viscerally disgusted by cheapness, yet another thing we agree on. If people are cheap with their money and their resources, they are also invariably cheap with their love. We believe that the more you give, the more it comes back to you. We have given out literally thousands of our books and done even more readings for people absolutely free as our service work. We genuinely like people, unless they show us that we are better off staying away from them, and we actually do seem to spread smiles and good cheer wherever we go. Our attitude is that life is short; we are all in this together, so let's have the best time possible under the circumstances. We have been privileged to have our actions validated by receiving so much caring and respect come back to us from the relatives that we do like, as well as from friends and even from strangers.

MONTE: GOOD ADVICE FROM MY PARENTS

When we got married, both my mother and my father came up to me— separately, of course—and told me the exact same thing. "Now that you are married, you have to put your wife and your marriage first." I was very pleased by this very good advice not just because it was something that I was going to do anyway, but because it was such selfless advice. In the years that passed, when we decided not to have children or when we could not visit as often as we would have liked because of our work schedules, I would remind my parents of their good advice and thank them genuinely for helping me to create the kind of relationship every good parent wants his or her child to have.

Remember, you are marrying *each other*, not each other's family, and you have to put your relationship first, above your allegiances to your family and your friends. If you want to know why Amy and I have an enchanted relationship, then you should know that not compromising our values just to placate someone else, especially those whose values we do not share, is certainly one of our most important secrets.

This is not to say that we do not care about what other people think. We are very solicitous of everyone we come in contact with. That is precisely why we have to be so selective of whom we spend time with. Caring about people who do not care for you and do not take you seriously enough to even listen to your point of view is a debilitating waste of time. It is better to spend your time helping those who care about you.

> Secret: **Respect yourself and show that same respect for others.** If you find it difficult to respect yourself, be aware that the most respectable people also have feelings of self-doubt. Self-doubt may never leave, but those who come to respect themselves learn to accept themselves as they are. Root out prejudiced ideas in yourself and be aware of them in others. Equal partners make successful relationships. There is no other way.

Ceremony: Preserving the Sacred

The wedding ceremony symbolizes to everyone that each of you is now more important to the other than anyone else. Creating your own marriage ceremony, complete with the traditions you respect and want to keep, as well as the traditions you would like to start, is creating a great work of art.

Ceremony helps us to make the cycles of our life more meaningful. It helps us to summon up all of our knowledge and to remember and enlist the help of the Divine. The use of ceremony shifts the levels of our perception and allows us to work in harmony with the cosmic forces. It reminds us that our powers are far greater than we sometimes realize. Such powers can create

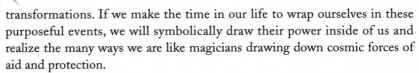

transformations. If we make the time in our life to wrap ourselves in these purposeful events, we will symbolically draw their power inside of us and realize the many ways we are like magicians drawing down cosmic forces of aid and protection.

When we visualize something in our mind's eye, we tell our Higher Self how we want our reality to materialize. If you want to add your Soul Mate to your life, you can visualize yourself being with that person, even if you do not know who she or he is yet. Create a silhouette in your mind into which this right person can come. You will be summoning your own unique powers, so don't think you have to follow our suggestions exactly. Be creative! Visualize your Soul Mate as a mountain, an animal, a favorite place, a smell, forces of weather, anything you like. Have fun with your visualizations. If it suits you, become a priestess or priest of your favorite religion and summon all that is good and holy in your faith to help you have a beautiful and sanctified marriage.

Amy and I have found that performing rituals on the Full Moon, a time of realization and fulfillment, or on the New Moon, a time of passage, rebirth, and beginning, makes them even more powerful. Performing a simple ritual in time to any of the Moon's cycles has been a sure way of linking up to forces empowering the human race since it first began. The Moon was the universal symbol for The Goddess, a reminder of its crucial significance as the first keeper of time and the seasons, a matter of life and death for those living off the land. Furthermore, when it was first realized that the Moon's cycle of twenty-nine and one-half days was mirrored in women's menstrual cycles, women were held sacred as nothing less than the living symbols of The Goddess. In the days when God was a woman, to harm a woman was an almost unthinkable crime of the utmost severity.

To properly perform a ritual ceremony you must know you are going to get what you concentrate on—what you bring into your full awareness. Surround yourself with beautiful things and reminders of the protection of divine forces as mediated by our Higher Selves.

Ceremony is used for the preservation of the sacred. Specific concepts are stored and communicated through elaborate iconography that imitates our connection to higher forces of creativity and light. Many of the traditions that have devolved into silly phrases and superstitions have their origin in a synthesis of all the fragments of human life, in order to create the totality our lives can become. That is why ceremonies themselves hold mystery with their hidden messages.

Ceremony regenerates our sense of our own possibilities and divinity. Its power alone can destroy self-doubt, the most daunting of the obstacles that inhibit our creative approach to living. Ceremony enhances the ritual of our daily life.

When a woman wears the clothes she has decided to be married in, whether they are from a thrift shop or one of Amy's incredible Goddess *Robes of Rapture*, she can become the essence of The Goddess. In marriage, both men and women can become the deep mystery of ultimate religious union, an experience that transcends concepts and explanations.

The ceremony renews our inner spirit whose source is the sacred. It reconciles order and chaos by connecting diverse patterns and materials that bridge space and time. Seemingly opposing concepts like Goddess and woman are brought into balance in keeping with the first alchemical principle: as above, so below. When we put on ceremonial clothing we are imitating our own spirit, which cloaks itself in different bodies at different times. It is a ritual that can remind us we come into the world naked and wear clothes until we are ready to be naked again after death, when we join the cosmos where there is no nakedness.

The important principle in every mythical drama is that the transformation taking place can be made visible through great art and ceremonies that acknowledge what we love. Though the alchemy of transformation, the significance of our life's lessons can be brought into our conscious minds.

MONTE: OUR BIG DAY

What with all the advice and caveats, I suppose you thought we'd never get around to telling you the story of our wedding. Well, here it is. A casual friend, Margie Dignan, most graciously (and unexpectedly) offered to us her very large, historic home in East Hampton for the day. We met her when I was doing sound reinforcement for a group of acrobats Margie was involved with. Her home at 63 Hunting Lane had the huge front and back lawns, several expansive porches and large rooms of the classic Hamptons summer "cottage" of the 1800s. It was a shingle-style Dutch roofed affair with a large in-ground pool with diving board and, befitting a woman who put on acrobatic plays, an in-ground trampoline. In short, it was the ultimate party house. We have always believed that when you need something and have faith, help will be offered. It sometimes comes disguised as something else, so you have to be attentive to and creative with what comes your way, but that is a lot more fun and good for your development than just having exactly what you want plopped in your lap. At any rate, this gorgeous house plopped into our laps, and we were—and are—very grateful.

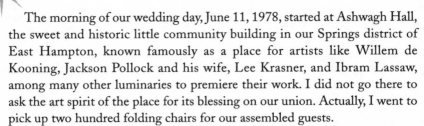

The morning of our wedding day, June 11, 1978, started at Ashwagh Hall, the sweet and historic little community building in our Springs district of East Hampton, known famously as a place for artists like Willem de Kooning, Jackson Pollock and his wife, Lee Krasner, and Ibram Lassaw, among many other luminaries to premiere their work. I did not go there to ask the art spirit of the place for its blessing on our union. Actually, I went to pick up two hundred folding chairs for our assembled guests.

After we set up the chairs, Amy and I hung about fifteen of her "Materializations," the exquisite fabric-collage tapestries for which she later won her NEA fellowship. We had happened to find more than a dozen silver lamé tablecloths in the Ladies' Village Improvement Society thrift shop. We festooned the tables with the flowers from the fifty rhododendrons from our garden that Jessie and Ray had planted when they all first moved to East Hampton. The place looked great.

I checked in with the catering staff, recruited from among our friends at the East Hampton Day Care Center, where Amy's sister, Toni, taught the cutest little kids. I made sure that the trays and trays of delicious mocha wedding cakes from Silver's restaurant in Southampton had arrived. Then I ran upstairs to change into my handmade, 1940s-vintage double-breasted wedding suit I bought from the Southampton Hospital thrift shop for ten dollars.

Amy's happy bridesmaids and our hairdresser, Jean, who left his chic Madison Avenue shop for the day in our honor, attended my beautiful bride. Her gorgeous wedding dress, a cream-colored lace 1940s-vintage stunner, was a two-dollar-fifty-cent "Scoresville" (as we call a great deal) from the same thrift shop where I'd gotten my suit.

At that time and for years afterward, we bought all of our clothes in thrift shops and lived on very little money. But you can have a lot of fun with a little money and we always did; we still do. Even now, when Amy's one-of-a-kind tapestry-embellished *Robes of Rapture* sell at New York City's Bergdorf Goodman for thousands and thousands of dollars, we still have fun shopping at flea markets for inspiring discoveries.

I love going shopping with Amy. I have recently had an insight into the phenomena of shopping. Shopping is like hunting and gathering. It is certainly different from when I accompanied my father and his police friends on hunting expeditions in the mountains of upstate New York, and for that I'm glad, but it satisfies that same primordial need to go out and hunt for what you want and need. If more men would realize this, I think they would not only be more understanding of their partner's need to shop, but would get into it enthusiastically, themselves, like I have done. Finding what you need for a great price is positively intoxicating.

Speaking of intoxicating, we had arranged to be married by our friend Jack, a psychiatrist who also happened to be an ordained minister. What we did not know was that he had given up a very long career of heavy drinking shortly before our wedding day. We attributed his demeanor and the tremor in his voice to nervousness at presiding over his first ceremony in many years. It was actually caused by having to do our ceremony sober. Happily, his sobriety has lasted since that time.

We met upstairs with Jack and our attendants—Amy's sister, Toni, and our friends Lori Solensten, Dan Romer, and John Okas. There we signed our marriage certificate. Then the whole lot of us went downstairs and did the wedding march from the side of the house up onto the steps of the front porch accompanied by music, my original compositions, played by Roland the Robot, my high-school-science-project-like musical sideman. Hmmm. Roland needs a bit of explaining.

I built Roland the Robot, a humanoid creature to accompany me when I plied my musician's trade in the local bars. I would prerecord several different parts on my huge reel-to-reel multitrack tape recorder, mix them down onto a cassette tape, and Roland, whose silver chest contained one of the first cassette tape recorders—about the size of a New York City phone book—would play it back while I accompanied myself on guitar, bass, flute, harmonica, or sometimes even sang a cappella. I called him Roland because his square head was the first electronic drum machine from the Roland Corporation, which I would use when all I needed was a drummer.

I called my futuristic one-man band, "The Me, My Sylph, and Eye Band," since a sylph is an imaginary being without a soul. Roland and I apparently did have soul and I am still asked about his whereabouts almost every month out here in the Hamptons. My joke about the whole thing was to say, truthfully, that my father had told me that if I kept wasting my life playing music, one day I would wake up and realize that I was thirty and that I had just been playing with myself.

One of the best things about having Roland as one of my three best men was that his arm was a microphone stand. Jack stepped up to it and read the vows we had written and passed out to the assembled happy throng. Here is a copy of our wedding vows:

> Our gathering here today is both a symbol and an example of love's power to bring people together. We have been asked here

to feel and to share in the mutual love of this man, Monte Farber, and this woman, Amy Rachel Zerner, and to witness their marriage celebration.

We live in a time where "science" and "religion" are finding a common ground in what once was known as "magic." Einstein proved that all matter is made of one kind of energy and that made us all relatives. Both we and the planets of our solar system are islands of matter adrift in oceans of time but, like all true relatives, the planets do have an influence on us.

We, too, have the power and the necessity to influence all things about us. Through watching the results of thoughts and deeds comes the realization that we get what we earn. For our every action there is a reaction that religion terms "The Law of Karma." According to this golden rule, it is not only a nice dream to be open to growth through positive thoughts and deeds, it is the most selfishly practical thing that we can do!

Our conditions in this life are a result of all that we have done as the many people we have been. Remembering this can give us strength and a tool with which to build a better tomorrow. Let us, then, renewing the past through the birth of our children, celebrate and dedicate to this future all our abilities for the good of all.

I have not read that since the day we were married and I must say that I am fairly astonished at how we have not changed what we believe or the voice in which we write. Neither of us thought of ourselves as writers at that time. I am certainly glad to be able to have shared our vows, our first collaborative effort, with you now.

We believe in short ceremonies and long parties so we kissed and said, "I do." Now married, we stayed on the porch as our 200 guests filed by congratulating, kissing, and hugging us before they walked into the living room where young Lisa Vetault and Judith Markowitz serenaded us on piano and flute. The delicious food disappeared and I must confess neither of us got to eat a crumb of wedding cake—it was so good that everyone had seconds before we had firsts! Of course, we were both floating a bit and fully satiated from two hundred kisses and hugs.

I had gotten to know a lot of musicians over the years and they all came and played at the wedding party. We had bluegrass on the pool porch, classical in the house, and rock-and-roll in the backyard. A flutist walked all over the place playing what has since come to be known as soothing New Age music to all and sundry. He backed up a healer doing the "laying on of hands" to a guest slightly injured on the trampoline. With all the music going on, there was a charged, celebratory feeling in the air.

My relatives, who still had not gotten over the fact that we were not being married in a traditional Jewish ceremony and by a rabbi, looked on in amazement as elegantly dressed guests of all ages bounced up and down on the trampoline, some bounding off only to dive into the adjacent pool fully clothed. It did get wild but never out of hand, though we did have a dozen or so party crashers.

In fact, the only wear and tear to the house and grounds came from our hostess who really got into the spirit of things and into the spirits, too. She was teaching Amy's blind eighty-year-old great-aunt how to shoot champagne corks over the roof onto the front lawn, where forty people were circling, holding hands, and calling up the "God Force."

The God Force was raised when everyone joined hands and prayed. We were helped in this endeavor from some of our friends whose Baptist heritage taught them that when the spirit moves you, you are going to shout, and shout we all did. We had forty people in a great circle on the front lawn and the electricity going through us was phenomenal, a great spiral of energy ascending to heaven. No one was surprised that we started receiving corks raining down on us, only we thought they were divinely produced and not the result of Great-aunt Jessie's new use for champagne, launching the ship of our married life.

We were so exhilarated that after everybody left, Amy and I changed into the vintage kimonos we'd received as gifts and cleaned the whole place up. My only regrets are that people were having too good a time to take a lot of pictures, and that I didn't have a picture of me at the dump unloading at least ninety-six empty champagne bottles off the truck right next to a fisherman, unloading a truckload of scallop shells. He smiled and shook his head, saying, "Must have been some party, Bub!"

Our enchanted marriage was off to an appropriately spiritual start. Picking the date astrologically worked as far as the weather was concerned, and as far as our life together has gone since. Yes, weddings have astrology charts, too, as do businesses, buildings, and anything else that gets created. People still tell us that ours was the best wedding they'd ever attended, and it only cost us two thousand dollars! Thanks to generous gifts from my father, my stepmother, Doris, and my uncle Morris and aunt Rosie, we were almost covered.

One of the funniest things about the whole event was that *Dan's Papers* reported it, complete with pictures of the wedding party and my robot best man, and though the paper is usually accurate, they spelled my name, "Merce Ferber." They spelled Amy and Roland's names correctly. The perfect end to a perfect day.

PART II

Lessons of Light

CHAPTER TEN

Lessons of Light:
An Oracle in a Book

*Make love your great quest; then desire spiritual gifts, and especially
that you may prophecy.*

—I CORINTHIANS 14:1

essons of Light" is not an ordinary book section. We have designed it
so that you can both read it like a book *and* use it as your own personal relationship oracle. It is here to offer you our continuing
guidance for the many decisions you have to make regarding the improving
of your relationships. We did it because we couldn't help ourselves; we make
oracles, we love oracles, we use oracles every day to help guide our own decisions, and we know how useful they can be for making practical improvements in our lives and our relationships.

For thousands of years, seekers wishing to act in harmony with divine
forces have consulted the oracles of the various gods and goddesses. An oracle can be defined as:

1. *The Answer* given since ancient times at a shrine as the response of the
goddess or god to an inquiry.

2. *The Medium* giving such responses.

3. *The Shrine* where these responses were given.

"Lessons of Light" combines all three of these things. It is your personal,
portable shrine dedicated to Love. It is also the medium through which you
can receive answers to your questions about bringing true love into your life
and keeping it there.

There are thirty-six "Lessons of Light" in this section. Each one is a
meditation designed to shine the light of your Higher Self on one aspect of
bringing true love into your life if you are alone, or improving an existing
relationship. When you use this section as an oracle, you will get guidance
from us and from your own intuitive faculties about how you can bring

more love into your life. It is a powerful way to make use of what you have learned from *Love, Light, and Laughter* on a daily basis. It is also a lot of fun.

For an oracle to be effective, it has to be comprehensive in scope and able to address *every* question you may have about love and relationships. For this reason, a few of the chapters in "Lessons of Light" contain advice that appears elsewhere in this book.

"Lessons of Light" is designed to give you advice that applies to your life in the real world and not just in the idyllic world of Soul Mates. A couple of the lessons, particularly "The Judge" and "The Actor," contain advice that might seem to run counter to the absolute honesty that the two of us share and know is essential to having an enchanted relationship. However, until you find your Soul Mate, you may find yourself in situations where total honesty and a lack of suspicion is not in your best interests. As the Bible says, "To every thing, there is a season and a time for every purpose under Heaven." These lessons of your gentle but powerful new oracle can guide you through the roughest of waters until you are safely ashore in your own enchanted world and beyond. Even Soul Mates need to keep secrets, like surprise parties and trips, and playing politics is often unavoidable to keep the peace with friends, relatives, and business associates.

As we say on the television shopping channels, "But wait, there's more!" "Lessons of Light" is not only an oracle. It can be used in a total of four ways:

1) You can read it straight through at your own pace.

2) You can skip around to whichever lesson's title strikes your fancy (another way of saying "gives your intuition a nudge"), until you have read them all.

3) You can contemplate one lesson a day for thirty-six days, keeping the book with you so that you can remember and apply that lesson in your life throughout your day.

4) You can use the pages of the "Lessons of Light" section as an oracle for answering the question "What do I need to know now about love and relationships for my highest good and greatest joy?" To do this, all you have to do is keep that question in your head as you open to one of the pages of this section at random. The page that you turn to will have the information that you need to hear at the time you ask your question. Even if only part of the answer resonates with you, the oracle has given you your message.

People have used this technique with the pages of the Bible for centuries to great success. Our religion is love, creativity, and spirituality and we have mixed all three together to help you reinforce the teachings in "Lessons of Light" in your daily life. Its concepts have become our relationship Bible.

Whichever way you decide to use the teachings of our "Lessons of Light," we have printed this book so that this section can be easily found. It can be seen as a dark section of pages when the book is closed and you look at it sideways.

The closest thing to an explanation of how and why oracles work is an ancient principle rediscovered in the twentieth century by pioneering psychologist Dr. Carl Jung. Dr. Jung called this principle "The Law of Synchronicity" (from the Greek *syn*, meaning "together," and *chronos*, meaning "time"). He noticed that things that happen at the same time can have a relationship of significance, if you know how to look at and decode the information. Dr. Jung postulated his theory of the "meaningful coincidence" (things that happen together in time) of outer and inner events to explain the accuracy of oracles, both the human oracles such as those at Delphi and that of divination systems, such as the ancient Chinese I Ching, the Norse runestones, the cards of our *Enchanted Tarot*, and the real astrology upon which our *Karma Cards* system is based. If the advice these inner guidance systems offered was not practical and useful, they would not have survived for thousands of years as they have done.

Like a hologram, each piece of the universe contains all the information necessary to re-create the whole universe. Throughout this limitless expanse, everything is connected to everything else. The interconnection and interdependence of all things is a basic premise of ancient wisdom, and it is a principle that has recently been proved mathematically by the new chaos theory, articulated by Benoit Mandelbrot. An oracle makes use of both our intuition and logical mind to receive and decode the information and then allows us to avail ourselves of it using a universal language we, and even the planets and stars, can understand.

For example, the practice of astrology results from millennia of observation during which astrologers noticed again and again meaningful coincidences between the positions of the planets and events taking place on Earth. Astrology has evolved into a language-like system that lets us "read" the positions of the planets at the moment of our birth. When we interpret the map of this frozen moment of time and space, we can gain valuable insights into our unique individuality. Using our personal astrological map or horoscope (from the Greek *hora*, "hour," and *skopos*, "to look at," literally "to look at the hour of birth") can make us aware of our strengths and weaknesses so that we may use our strengths to compensate for our weaknesses.

Like the movement of the planets, synchronicity never seems to stop. Like gravity, no one knows exactly why it works, but it certainly does work. Synchronicity is as common as gravity; when you look for it, you see it everywhere.

Each of the thirty-six "Lessons of Light" also have an *affirmation* for you to use as one of the ways to reinforce the teaching you are concentrating on in your life.

We all use affirmations every day, both positive, like "I can do that," and negative, like "I cannot do that because I'm too weak, dumb, fat, skinny, poor, and so forth," or any of the hundreds of other reasons we come up with for why we aren't living the life we want and deserve. Ever since we first started living together, Amy and I have found that setting aside a time each morning for repeating positive affirmations helps to undo the effects of negative affirmations and helps us to become aware when we are lapsing into using them. As the philosopher G. I. Gurdijeff said, "When falling asleep wakes you up, you know you are making progress."

Synchronicity not only explains how astrology works and how the tarot and all of the other divination systems that we have created work, but also how we met and how you, too, can meet your Soul Mate and live in an enchanted world. First, remember that you do live in an enchanted world. You may think it anything but an enchanted world, but try looking at all the magic in your life, starting with the breath that gives you life. There are so many miracles, if you are willing to stop spending your precious time looking at what is wrong with your world and start looking at what is truly amazing. Be grateful for what you have. Try to recapture your childlike sense of wonder about things. You do not have to walk around wide-eyed at everything and have people start worrying about you, but let your natural enthusiasm and curiosity emerge. Soon, you will start to feel that your life is actually connected to all life in a positive way.

"Lessons of Light" is a new map for the new millennium. When you look at today's high divorce rate and the growing number of people raising their children in single-parent households, you can see the often harsh consequences for people who feel they have grown beyond their partnership and have decided not to settle for less than the kind of loving relationship they feel they deserve. In these exciting, challenging, and turbulent times, people are seeking true love, comfort, and reassurance in their relationships, and those without a partner are seeking one with an urgency greater than usual. "Lessons of Light," as a unique kind of map and guidebook, can enable Soul Mates to find each other, even today when the world seems to be as dark as a cloudy night.

Affirmation:
*I ask for what I want
because I deserve to get
what I want.*

Lesson 1. The Warrior

How well do you express your own needs? How much of your time, energy, and other resources do you allow a partner to demand of you? Problems you are experiencing with your love life may be the result of your not asking either your partner, others, or even your Higher Self to give you what you are entitled to have. You may have a tendency to give too much of yourself and to ask too little of your partner in return. You may be more comfortable living both for the significant other person in your life and living through them.

Too many people erroneously believe that love requires giving of yourself selflessly without expecting anything in return. One can only feel unsatisfied by this kind of relationship, for it is not true love. In your heart, you know the loving relationship you seek is one where you and your partner give and receive from each other in equal measure. For this to happen, you must first identify what you really want for yourself and then ask for it clearly and directly, knowing you deserve to get what you want and need.

When you practice standing up for yourself, the way Warriors do, you will finally see things come into harmony in many aspects of your life. You will be in a much better position to either improve your current relationship greatly or find a new one that will bring you much peace and joy.

Problems you may have now regarding your love life may be caused by the fact that you are afraid that a loving relationship will require you to give up your own life with your own hopes, dreams, and desires. So you resist doing what you know you must do to bring this kind of a loving relationship into your life.

It may be true that your past experience caused you to feel smothered and imprisoned by what you thought was love. But by changing your definition of what a loving relationship means to you into something you know you can live with, you allow your Higher Self to bring such a relationship into your life.

Affirmation:

*I enjoy my life now as I
realize my hopes and wishes.*

Lesson 2. The Jeweler

Sometimes everything is going just as it should be, even if it doesn't appear that way on the surface. Some of the problems you may be experiencing in your relationship are really there for your own good! At some time in the near or distant past, you were very helpful to another person with their love situation. Remember that you will reap the rewards of your good deeds. Your good luck may be manifesting in a way that seems to be making your life more hectic and confrontational on many fronts. Do not despair. Your difficulties are pointing out areas in your life that need work.

If you find your partner or someone you are interested in does not want to do the work necessary to make your relationship grow stronger, you should be thankful that you are finding out now while you still have time to do something about it. If there is no one in your life right now, the love you will soon experience will be worth waiting for. By realizing present difficulties are for the best, you manifest the positive attitude that can bring a wonderful relationship to you.

Your greatest challenge now is to maintain a positive attitude when things do not appear to be going the way you want them to. As long as you continue to act and react properly, your positive outcome is virtually assured. However, if you find yourself in any dangerous or dishonest situations, you must do everything in your power to get out of them. You do not want to waste the powerful good luck you have worked so hard to attain. The same energies that would have to be spent keeping you out of harm's way could bring you a fabulous love life if you let them.

Act as if good things are on the way. The ancient sages knew that our beliefs about reality mold and shape our experience of reality. And so you are challenged to relinquish all limiting beliefs about yourself and believe that you are going to get the wonderful love relationship you have always dreamed of. It may come to you in a surprising way, but it will come to you. In fact, it is on its way right now. All you have to do is follow your heart, taking small steps forward on your path, and do what you know is right. The patient Jeweler saves his best attention for the finest jewel.

Affirmation:

I have the right to speak and be taken seriously because I am respectful and attentive when others speak.

Lesson 3. The Storyteller

In order to bring love into your life or improve an existing relationship, it is important that you enable others to better understand you by informing them of the people and events that have helped to make you who you now are. Your challenge is to tell your tale in a way that is interesting to both you and to your listener. This is not as easy as it can seem when a skillful Storyteller tells a story. However, by turning your attention to this task, you will gain a perspective on your life and communication skills that you may now be lacking. This, in itself, can have a powerfully positive effect on your love life.

The art of storytelling is useless without the art of listening, and so you must remember to listen to your partner when he is speaking. Make sure you are really listening and not just appearing to do so as you think about what you are going to say next. Whether you are interacting with someone you have just met or talking to your mate of twenty years, there are few things as attractive about a person as someone who is interested in what you are saying. Interest leads to sharing and sharing leads to caring.

Conversely, there are few things as annoying as someone who does not listen to what you are saying or does not take you seriously. If you and your partner are not interested in what you have to say to each other, you are not really interested in each other. You may be involved in a relationship based on practical considerations or on physical attraction alone. Not being heard can lead to your feeling misunderstood and not appreciated for who you really are.

In storytelling, it is crucial to be aware of your audience. Therefore, as you examine your life in the presence of one important to you, ask questions about her life with a mind toward finding similar or related situations. When storytelling leads to mutual examination and personal exploration, it creates a close bond of understanding that deepens love and begins the work of enchantment.

Affirmation:
I deserve to feel safe and nurtured because I give loving care and acceptance to those I cherish.

Lesson 4. The Nurturer

You and your lover must demonstrate to each other that you are capable of giving and receiving unconditional love. You must both feel you can trust one another completely and can turn to each other for strength, support, and gentle guidance when one partner feels hurt or otherwise weakened.

Look inside yourself and see if you are suppressing your maternal instincts when in the presence of the one you are supposed to care for. One or both of you may feel uncomfortable displaying this aspect of your personality, or you may feel it does not exist in you. If this is so, there are several reasons that could be causing you to feel this way about something that exists in us all, including men.

If your experience of the one who mothered you was unpleasant, or if no one fulfilled your need for nurturing, protection, and unconditional love, you would not be clear about how to do so for another. Or you might think that "mothering" and "smothering" are the same.

You might be reluctant to show your nurturing side to anyone who seems independent for fear you would be rejected. Those who project an image of independence at all costs often desperately need support but are too proud or unaware of their neediness to ask. They act out their frustrations in the same way they did as children when they didn't get what they needed. The child we were still lives within us. Only now, as adults, we are capable of causing a lot more trouble for ourselves and others if we ignore the fact that we all need nurturing.

Be a Nurturer, and seek one. Like a mother with a stubborn child, sometimes you must just wade in and break through this wall of feigned independence and reach that child within who is calling out for help. If you you care about someone worthy of your energy, make sure that he can pass this test: either he's already nurtured you or you feel certain he will when you need it. Even the best of mothers has a hard time giving selflessly when her own needs have not been fulfilled.

Affirmation:
I know how to lead because I know what needs to be done.

Lesson 5. The Leader

There are times when your ability to assume a position of authority and control is crucial for bringing true love into your life or for improving an existing relationship. Sometimes you have to be the one who volunteers to organize the situation for the benefit of all. When it's obvious that you are being called upon to take control of your life—especially your love life—you must lead, not just with words, but also by your example. If you think you cannot lead until you know exactly what to do, it is time you learned the truth about all great Leaders: they do the best they can.

If you are in a relationship in which something needs to be done, you sometimes have to be the smart one. If you have pointed out the issues and planned solutions with your partner, but nothing happens, then do it yourself. If you wait for your partner to take the lead, you may be disappointed. Even if she appears resistant to taking your direction, in her heart of hearts she knows you're right, and she'll come around to your way of thinking sooner than you think. Your partner's inaction may be justified in some way. He may be overcommitted or distracted. It's also possible that he might be confused and have lost his way. This happens to everybody sometimes.

There are times when your partner needs to feel secure by knowing you can provide strong leadership. Power is said to be the ultimate aphrodisiac. By displaying the power to take command at the appropriate time, you enhance your attractiveness.

If you're looking for a loving relationship, cultivate an air of confidence and trustworthiness. In everything you do, don't take shortcuts or get involved with any underhanded activities. Behave nobly and with great style, no matter what economic class you were born into. When you're the Leader, you must temporarily put your own needs second to that of your relationship. At the same time, be careful to avoid seeming overbearing and dictatorial. Let your good example be the best sermon. It is especially important to avoid cheap shots or pettiness. Many people have a hard time accepting direction from someone who does not live up to a very high set of standards.

Monte Farber & Amy Zerner

Affirmation:
*I enjoy being alone and
getting in touch with who I
am as an individual.*

Lesson 6. The Worker

S ometimes you'll need to examine your words, thoughts, feelings, and actions to make sure that you are not focusing too much of your attention on your relationship. Sometimes you need to focus more on your work and career, even your hobbies. It is as practical to stop micromanaging your relationship as it is to focus on financial and other worldly considerations.

If you are trying too hard to improve an existing relationship, take a break from it. As our friend, noted psychiatrist and guided imagery pioneer, Gerald Epstein, M.D., says in *Healing Into Immortality*, it is time to "separate your attention from your intention." This advice holds true for accomplishing all goals. You may be surprised at the positive results you see in your relationship when you forget for a while. Perhaps you have been overly concerned about it or your partner has noticed your concern and isn't so happy about it. Focusing all that energy on other things for a while will allow you to be yourself again. Be a Worker in the world. It will at least give you a new perspective when, and if, you return to "working" on your relationship. Your break from doing so may offer a fresh perspective later.

If you are trying to bring a loving relationship into your life, consider the logic of this advice: Assume there is someone out there for you and let it go at that. You do not have to do anything to make things happen. If you find yourself with unsatisfying people and relationships, it is possible that, as of now, you're not yet the person your Soul Mate is looking for. It is possible that by focusing on your career, you will become that person. You may develop skills, resources, and attitudes resulting from your work experiences, which will help you develop your authentic self.

By completely forgetting about your romantic potential for a while, you may very well project your most attractive qualities to the kind of person you have been seeking for so long. It is worth a try. By not fearing solitude, you exhibit a very attractive strength.

Affirmation:
I love life and I love my life.

Lesson 7. The Lover

If the purpose of life is to be happy, then remember that life is a party to be enjoyed to the best of your ability (as long as you remember, "Nothing in excess"). You don't need to go out of your way to encounter the delights of romance. Your lust for life will make you very attractive. You would do best to make yourself, your possessions, and your surroundings as attractive and impressive as possible and thereby draw to you what you have been searching for. To strive and strain in obvious effort to attain romance works against you. Be in the moment, experiencing a readiness for romance with a gentle purity.

Spend some time with fun, attentive, and even flirtatious people. There is nothing wrong if you enjoy believing the wonderful things you are hearing and feeling as long as you do not go overboard and change your life because of them. Flirtations may be a one-time encounter or lead to a lifelong commitment. The important thing is to have some fun, so put thoughts of the future out of your mind for now. Worry and analysis can kill the delicate blossom of a budding relationship. The present moment needs and deserves your full attention. Let the future wait and take care of itself.

Though you may very well have met your Soul Mate, put such thoughts out of your head for now and just concentrate on putting your best foot forward. Talk of marriage kills the mood. Be charming and cultivate a sense of humor about everything, without being glib or silly. It is not a time for heavy discussions about the affairs of the world. Romantic affairs are more important now, and you should let them claim your attention. There will be time for matters of global importance later.

Though you would do well not to take any foolish action you would regret later, grant yourself permission to take a break from worry and pragmatism and logic. Let a little romance into your life, even if you have to do it yourself with a trip to a place you love. That place can be across the street or around the world, as long as it makes you feel romantic. Be a Lover of that time and place, which gives you practice being a Lover for the time when your Soul Mate is your object.

If you are in an existing relationship, both of you should try to recover the indescribable excitement and exhilaration that comes with the first blush of romance. It should be fun, not work or a sacred duty. A relationship incapable of recapturing that feeling risks boredom and failure.

Affirmation:

I am relentless in my pursuit of justice.

Lesson 8. The Judge

When things in a relationship go wrong, the necessary big changes are often frightening and confusing. But you must act according to what you know is true or what you come to know, in spite of your fears. At times like that, you must face up to things the way they really are, not as you would like them to be. Things may change for the better but they will not change unless you ruthlessly judge yourself and your situation and act accordingly when the time is right and not before.

For example, if you suspect that someone may be lying to you or judging you wrongly, then you must find out whom, why, and how. Once you do, you can confront the offender with your truth, stated clearly and calmly. An effective Judge waits to issue her opinion until she's gathered all the facts, but once she does, her judgment tolerates no further deceit. Until you are absolutely sure of yourself, do not act differently from your normal routine and do not volunteer information, even to your closest friends. You may have to skirt the truth in order to combat the wrong that is being done to you. This is why it is very important that you are absolutely sure of your situation before you act.

It is time to become aware of how the art of seduction is practiced. Cultivating an air of mystery would be a good way to regain control of the situation. Display the qualities of the strong, silent type to the best of your ability. If you must talk, whisper.

It might be a good idea to read a good detective story to refresh your memory about how a good detective has to think and act. There is a need for self-control in order to dominate the situation. If caution is not exercised, there is the danger that you may find yourself dominated by another. Judgment has its time and place. Your judgment is a gift meant to protect you.

And if it's you, yourself, who warrants judgment, if, for example, you are involved in a relationship reduced to a debilitating power struggle, an obsessive nightmare, or a petri dish for violence, you have to abide by the decision of your own interior Judge and begin to take actions calculated to change things immediately. It is likely that you will have to make a clean break. If professional counseling fails to help, you should call in the power of social service workers, the police, and the judicial system to protect your interests, especially if children are involved.

Affirmation:
I know how to act in this situation.

Lesson 9. The Actor

L ife is a game, and games have rules. You probably already know that everyone forgets the Golden Rule sometimes, so you must learn to protect yourself from thoughtless actions.

Often in life things are not what they seem to be. Most likely, however, appearances rather than people are doing the deceiving. In any case you must question your assumptions about everything. It will not be enough to trust that things are still the same just because you do not see how they have changed.

Sometimes appearances are important and style is as important as substance. If you are in a relationship where your partner is either unwilling or incapable of accepting things the way they are, you have to choose between being honest with him or her or playing a bit of a game, being a bit of an actor. For example, you may have to pretend that you have more or less money or possessions than you really have. In order to assist in this transitional time, it's important to stay in your role until it's clear that all concerned can handle the stress involved. If it becomes obvious your partner is never going to be able to handle the stress of the truth, then you will have to leave.

It's often been said that the theater is a dictatorship, with the director acting in that role. No wonder actors are legendary for knowing how to play politics. It's time for you to learn the craft of acting.

Acting was one of the three holy arts of ancient India, because an actor imitates the Divine Spirit when he brings a character to life in a drama. Furthermore, the ancient sages knew a powerful technique for achieving goals: how to act as if one already has the desired goal. Sometimes you should act and, most importantly, feel as if things are the way you would like them to be. This will alert and inform your powerful subconscious mind about how you would like things to be. You may then begin to see that things start moving in that direction as if by magic. It may also become clear to you that you need to readjust your priorities and your life.

Affirmation:
I study and share wisdom with one who is wise and experienced enough to value it.

Lesson 10. The Teacher

W hen the fire of first meeting diminishes, your partner's intellect will become increasingly important to you. Even if looks, sexual compatibility, and shared activities formed the basis for your early acquaintance, at some point you will find your partner's intelligence and manner of expressing it either wonderful or worrisome. If you find yourself in a relationship that does not satisfy you intellectually, you must try to do something to put it on track.

The desire to improve our lives is one of our most basic needs. One of the best ways to improve an existing relationship is to improve yourself. Devoting time to self-improvement, by way of self-directed study or a class or study group, will enable you to change your situation for the better in many ways.

If you are interested in someone who seems to be a serious person, then it is important to behave in as mature, learned, and wise a way as you are capable of. Even your appearance should be that of a serious person who wants to learn more. Basing your actions on what is "normal," expected and accepted behavior, tradition, research, facts, and figures will give you the best results. Obviously, a relationship like this might start through a meeting in a library, museum, school, theater, or other place of culture and learning. If people of your own age or social circle do not seem mature or interesting enough, you might want to consider looking for someone older, more experienced, or wiser than you. You might truly enjoy being in a position to learn from a brilliant partner who respects and treasures you as a wise-person in training. If that sounds unattractive to you, then consider playing the role of teacher to your next love interest. This might require being with someone younger than you, but not necessarily.

The dynamic of all relationships fluctuates, regardless of how each began. One partner may act as the teacher for a time, or around a particular issue, and the other assumes the role of student. Or one partner may "parent" the other and vice versa. This is as it should be. Soul Mates are everything to each other: lover, best friend, partner, child, parent, and teacher.

Affirmation:
*I am my Soul Mate's
best friend.*

Lesson 11. The Friend

How you feel about friendship can sometimes determine the quality of your relationship. Of course, most people enjoy the company of their friends, but the issue here is how you feel about friendship inside a romantic relationship.

If you are involved in a relationship with someone who has no friends, or who obviously values their friends more than you, or if your friendship is not as valued as the status, goods, and services you provide, the chances are very likely this relationship will not last long. Even if a relationship somehow endures without friendship, it is never completely satisfying, no matter what other needs it may serve. No matter how good the physical chemistry or how exciting the courtship, when the intoxication of the early days fades, trouble will start. The odds are that someone was more infatuated with the high octane of a new romance rather than with the person himself. Soul Mates are each other's best friends, without exception.

If you are seeking to bring true love into your life, don't dismiss the possibility that it may come through an introduction through friends or through a platonic friendship. No matter if it is someone you already know or someone you have yet to meet, the important thing is whether or not the relationship is built on the solid foundation of mutual respect.

You may not be physically attracted to a friend at first. This is a perfectly natural self-defense mechanism because we all fear rejection and are well aware that a romantic relationship can ruin a good friendship.

Be careful if you display the all-too-common tendency to think that someone who is nice and kind is weak and boring. Too many people are looking for excitement because they think that's what love is. Real love is exciting because the two of you care so much about each other and show it in every way. To equate excitement with dangerous, inconsiderate, or obsessive behavior is to invite disaster into your life.

If you are not with someone, don't try to decide which of your old or new friends is going to be your next relationship. Like friendship, any new relationship is going to grow at its own pace based upon many factors, both known and unknown.

Affirmation:

I have faith in my ability to act in harmony with my highest principles to help myself and others.

Lesson 12. The Healer

Sometimes you'll find it necessary to go beyond parental roles and give your partner what she really wants, not what you think she needs. As long as you honor your beliefs about right and wrong, and even though you may not agree with her, your relationship should have room for this kind of generosity. Finding love or improving an existing relationship requires active work and faith. Faith is the belief in things unseen. There is always the risk that your faith in another may turn out to have been unfounded, but you must follow your heart and your head and try if it seems the thing to do.

You may meet your future Soul Mate in the performance of a charitable act. Before you make any personal sacrifice to advance the interests of another, however, please consider all your motives in order to determine if such philanthropy is warranted. Focusing on the needs of others is noble work, but don't let it be an escape from loneliness or from the urgent, competitive side of life. The all too human tendency to idealize another whom we love past logic can sometimes be the result of deception or lack of self-worth. This can set us up for disappointment. You must be strong and relatively secure to give strength to others. In other words, you must heal yourself before you can help others heal.

In an existing relationship that has otherwise been going well, there are times that you must have pity on yourself or your partner. There are times when you must be the one to make peace. At those times, lead the way in the exploration of healing practices designed to cure problems on the physical, mental, and spiritual levels.

If you seek a loving relationship, you may find it with someone markedly more or less fortunate than you in some way. This can work out fine, but it's an unfortunate human trait to resent helpers and healers, especially if the helper has done most of the work. Do not worry. If you are willing to take on the big work of being Soul Mates, resentment issues should resolve themselves.

Affirmation:

I use my intuition to guide my rational mind to make the perfect decision.

Lesson 13. Intuition

There will be times in your life, especially your love life, when you will have to make split-second decisions. In our case, we would not have found each other back in 1974 had we not made lots of quick decisions the night of our double date at the overcrowded Patti Smith concert in chapter 8.

We all make decisions the same way, scrambling to gather as much information as we can, delaying our decision until we absolutely have to, and then—we guess. If we are lucky, we won't have waited too long. Some call it going by their "gut instinct" or "flying by the seat of their pants." We call it listening to our intuition.

Intuition is your natural inner guidance system, the small, quiet voice within us that is always trying to tell us what is in our best interests. Even when we are ignoring it, our intuition is always doing its job. We all can hear it when we are calm and quiet. The trouble is that we do not pay it respectful attention. We must use both our intuition and rational mind in harmony to make full use of our decision-making abilities.

The common denominator of all the problems caused by people is poor decision making. It is easy to blame our problems and failures on other people and circumstances beyond our control. It is more difficult, but more rewarding, to take responsibility for where your decisions have brought you. If your decisions have brought you here, making better decisions will lead you to where you want to go, including to an enchanted relationship.

The best way we have found to harmonize our rational and intuitive faculties is with the daily use of oracles. The oracles we've presented here, rooted in ancient wisdom, are consciously designed to help you develop your intuition for better decision making here in the twenty-first century.

Throughout this book, we have tried to appeal to your rational mind about love, a subject that most people think is the most irrational emotion there is. We know we are up against ingrained, centuries-old, misinformed views about love and so we send out a wall of truth and our secret techniques, knowing full well that a few people will still just sit there and say, "But I *love* the jerk!" even when they are obviously with the wrong person. The reason they think they love the jerk is that they do not really know or want to know what love is, though their intuition has been trying to tell them for years.

Affirmation:
I think positively and manifest the bright future that I see in my mind's eye.

Lesson 14. Manifestation

The ability to use affirmations and visualizations for manifesting our desires is one of the most important secrets we have. The results only seem like magic; in truth, we all have the same incredible power to work such changes.

When we use affirmations or visualize something in our mind's eye, we tell our Higher Self how we want our reality to materialize. If you want to be with your Soul Mate, visualize yourself being with that person, even if you do not know who he or she is yet. See him or her as a silhouette or as someone you know or know of and are attracted to and know that the right person is going to come into your life. You are summoning your own unique power so do not think that you have to use our suggestions as your guide. Be creative! Visualize your Soul Mate as a mountain, an animal, a favorite place, smell, weather, anything that you like. Have fun with your visualizations. If it suits you, become a priestess or priest of your favorite religion in your visualization and summon all that is good and holy in your faith to help you have a beautiful and sanctified marriage.

Manifestation is a practice that requires you to decide what you want and then visualize it, seeing it not only with your inner sight, but feeling it as if you were really there, experiencing it with all of your senses. At first it will be difficult to practice your visualization even once a day, but you'll get better—work up to several times a day.

Whenever you find yourself drifting back into old patterns of negative thinking, don't get mad, get even. Just smile at the tenacity of this nasty habit struggling to stay alive inside your head and know you have the power to defeat it. Then go back to visualizing what it is you want with all your heart.

If guided mental imagery can help you manifest what you like, it should come as no surprise that daily visualization of what you do *not* like will, unfortunately, help you manifest that as well. That is why it is so important for you to think positively. It is more than wishful thinking! Visualization is part of a comprehensive and proven plan for changing your life for the better.

Affirmation:
*I communicate clearly
and easily.*

Lesson 15. Communication

The difficulties we have with other people usually result from communication problems. Our ability to communicate is often the key to bringing true love into our life or making an existing relationship better. Most often, problems arise because the parties involved are not making themselves clear, or someone (or both) is refusing to really listen. It is a waste of everyone's time to let fear and preconceived notions stand in the way of real communication.

Proper communication begins with an effort to make yourself clearly understood and to understand how your partner communicates. It is important to remember that the same words can often mean different things to different people. This disconnect can be the result of cultural, regional, and age differences. A person's life experiences can attach very specific meanings, both positive and negative, to words and situations others would experience neutrally.

For this reason, you must read body language as well as speech in order to get a whole sense of what your beloved is saying. Look into the eyes of someone you are interested in relating to. If your partner is looking or leaning away and has folded his arms across his chest, you can pretty much guarantee that what you're saying is making him feel defensive or uncomfortable. Sighing or slouching can indicate sadness. You know what yawning means!

When such a reaction registers with you, wait for an opening in the conversation and ask your partner directly if what you've said is making her uncomfortable. This question will display your concern and can give you immediate feedback about how she feels with this much openness and intimacy. What you discover can lead to further exchanges, or show you that you might have to look for your Soul Mate elsewhere.

Always remember that if you are interested in a person, let your interest be known in a way that both of you are comfortable with. It is amazing how interesting someone becomes when we realize he is genuinely interested in us; you may have to be that obvious.

If all of your efforts to establish a genuine dialog with your partner seem to come to naught, or if he refuses to speak to you as a form of punishment, you'll definitely have to look elsewhere for your Soul Mate. Sometimes what passes for the strong, silent type is really someone with nothing to say.

Affirmation:
I forgive myself and everyone else with compassion for our human frailties.

Lesson 16. Forgiveness

There must be forgiveness, both of yourself and others, in order for healing and love to dwell within your heart. The energy you might otherwise channel into thoughts of revenge will only work against you on many levels. Make any potential partners aware of the fact that you know how to forgive.

Close your eyes to the irritating behavior of another if you are sure both in head and heart that she is worthy of your forgiveness and that such an exercise of compassion will help her to grow. Growing pains are a fact of life not only on the physical level, but on mental, emotional, and spiritual levels as well.

Problems that manifest in our lives are often a result of problems we have been unable to resolve on these nonphysical levels. If we resist growing more fully into who we really are and refuse to see the wisdom of changing our outmoded beliefs and attitudes, we will find ourselves in physical world situations that force us to confront what was once an inner conflict. When that happens, we can either grow, or retreat from the pain and suffering that inevitably accompanies growth.

Forgiveness is the antidote to the poison of blame. All too often, we tend to blame rather than try to solve the problem. Blaming someone else provides only false comfort to the blamer. If both of you in a relationship are trying to grow, the odds are pretty good that you'll both make the sort of mistake that will beg for forgiveness. It is not weakness but the greatest strength to forgive.

Every night before you go to sleep, forgive everyone: yourself, your parents, your siblings, your other relatives, friends, coworkers, ex-spouses or lovers, and anyone else who has wronged you. It will not only help you to soothe the hurt in your heart, but you will sleep better, too. Accept your human frailty and everyone else's as a natural part of human fallibility, and your mistakes as a sign of your efforts to grow. If you are not failing, you are not trying. The time of failure is the best time to plant the seeds of success.

Affirmation:
I love playing the game of life creatively.

Lesson 17. Creativity

When you are already in a relationship or are working to bring true love into your life, you must be playful and enjoy life every day. Having fun is not wasted time. Make time in your busy life to simply play without looking for results. Not only is love a game, life itself is a game, too. To demean the importance of games and fun is to demean the importance of life. The refreshing joy, exhilaration, and skills gleaned from play can help you solve your problems, especially problems with your love life.

If you and your partner share an interest in the same sport or other recreational activity, try it together. If, despite this shared interest, one of you prefers to be alone or to share these activities with other friends, it may signal a problem in your relationship. Soul Mates love to be together.

Explore your creative talents. Creativity is equal parts intelligence, intuition, and heroism. Intelligence lets you examine and understand the problem, intuition comes as insightful solutions, and heroism girds you to implement your idea.

The challenge is to recapture the sense of adventure, wonder, and playfulness of a child. Children see a situation, ask questions, and come up with completely fresh ideas. Playing with pets and creating pet names for each other can help you recapture childlike joy and innocence.

Play this little game and your reward will be true love. Look at your relationship as if you are seeing it for the first time. Question everything without fearing that you will bring up answers you may not like. What is really going on? How is it affecting you and your potential ideal love? If you could wave a magic wand and make anything happen, how would you want things to be? What is preventing things from being that way? What, if anything, can be done to eliminate the obstacles in your way? Take a chance on new things, especially the ones that sound like fun.

Affirmation:
*I can handle whatever
life brings me now and
in the future.*

Lesson 18. Worry

It is easy to see that how you deal with worry and criticism is crucial to your love life. We must have faith that we can handle whatever comes, including criticism from those we love and respect. Otherwise, you'll get stuck in obsessiveness and compulsive behavior, both of which are real threats to true love.

When you worry, you feel that things are not the way they should be. Our expectations and attachment to outcomes make us hold ourselves and others hostage to arbitrary standards.

There is an important difference between analysis and criticism. Analyzing a situation is an important step in making things better. However, anxiety holds us rigidly in place, preventing relationships from growing, particularly when we yearn to know the perfect plan or the outcome of plans and actions before they have reached fruition. There's always an unknown in every situation, and we have to embrace its wild card possibilities in order to live a full life.

When we look back on what we used to worry about, it's almost comic to see that most of our past anxiety was a waste of time. We usually deal more or less successfully with whatever circumstances arise. We *have* to. At its core, worry is a natural desire to protect yourself from pain by anticipating problems. However, you'll be taking a much more practical and logical approach if you let your successes rather than your failures transform your life. It's powerful to focus on your accomplishments and achievements!

To endure the imperfection in all things demonstrates a realistic understanding of the material world. Reserve criticism only for constructive purposes, rather than hiding behind its smoke screen to belittle and blame. Destructive criticism is little more than a misguided attempt to deflect criticism away from oneself onto another.

Receiving criticism is an art. If you react poorly to criticism, you prevent even the most constructive kind from benefiting you. If you always react negatively to criticism, think about that, and see if you might instead be responding to old, unfounded fears. Even the most basic adjustments to thinking and communications can avoid hurtful misunderstandings.

Affirmation:
I love you.

Lesson 19. Love

We tell each other how much we love each other all the time. We have come to realize that doing so is one of the most powerful and enchanting of our many secrets. Saying, "I love you," to each other is not only pleasant to say and hear, it is an empowering affirmation of the most important truth in our life.

If you are not with someone, then say, "I love you." to yourself. You cannot love another unless you love yourself. If you are with someone, tell her you love her. If you don't love her, why are you with her? You know you have found your Soul Mate when you enjoy just watching her live; when your desire to make your partnership work causes you both to want to be there for each other in every way. What distinguishes love from romance, sexual attraction, friendship, service, or any other aspect of life is that love contains them all and in their highest, most beautiful expression.

Romance is exhilarating because it brings out the best in you but also because it is usually brief. Sexual attraction can be so urgent that it can overwhelm reason. Friendship and service and healing and everything else positive and life-affirming are all wonderful and also have their important place in your life. However, when you love someone and he loves you, all these things and more combine in a way you cannot imagine until it happens to you. Your lover is your friend and yet romance is only a glance away. Sexual attraction is heightened rather than frightened away by mutual intimacy, trust, and commitment. When you love someone, you want to be with him as much as possible because at long last you have found him and life's brevity becomes starkly apparent. Soul Mates work on their relationship by working on themselves.

Affirmation:

I transform myself and my relationship as a caterpillar transforms into a butterfly.

Lesson 20. Transformation

Sometimes how you feel about change—especially your ability to change yourself and your situation—is crucial to your being able to bring true love into your life or make an existing relationship better.

Change and transformation are inevitable. They can lead to destruction, but they can also lead to growth. We have found that if you don't grow together, you grow apart, and in more ways than one. Though we have said many times that it's impossible to change someone who doesn't yet want to change, sometimes when your partner notices a change in you and envies your results, she might overcome her own rigidity and look for ways to improve her lot, too. But you can't wait forever for her to come around.

If you decide you would like things in your relationship to be different, you pose a threat to the status quo. However, a relationship incapable of changing is dying or dead. The surest sign of life in the natural world is growth and movement. By even intuiting the need for change, you have begun the process. Be brave and press forward, even if you're unclear about the outcome of your efforts.

If you wish to bring true love into your life, then you will do well to learn about the power of prayer. Prayer is a form of magic in which we seek to ally ourselves with what some call the Divine. Prayer puts us in mental and spiritual harmony with supremely powerful forces. Opening yourself to the unseen in this way unleashes your power as a spiritual being, for whom all things are possible.

Ceremony helps us to make the cycles of our life more meaningful. It helps us to summon all of our knowledge and to remember and enlist the help of the Divine. The use of ceremony shifts the levels of our perception and allows us to work in harmony with the cosmic forces. It reminds us that our powers are far greater than we sometimes realize. Such powers can create transformations. If we make the time in our life to wrap ourselves in these purposeful events, we will symbolically draw their power inside of us and realize the many ways we are like magicians drawing down cosmic forces of aid and protection.

Affirmation:

*I expand my awareness
about what is possible.*

Lesson 21. Awareness

Learning and travel expand your awareness of possibilities and will help you bring true love into your life or make an existing relationship better. A wise person makes the time to build on what has come before and to find ways to make a better future. You must know you want things to get better before they can. But to make the most of the energies available for improvement, you have to do your homework and see how the rest of the world lives.

If you are in a relationship you want to improve, try travel, especially to places that show you new and different ways of being and thinking free from your everyday routine. Traveling to see familiar people, places, and things isn't as enlightening, but sometimes even the fully aware trip across the street can reveal new insights about living.

The technological marvels of our time give us almost limitless ways to obtain useful information from the best sources. Travel, education, publishing, communication systems, the Internet, and broadcasting can bring the world to us. Attend the lectures and workshops of visiting experts, go to school, read, or use interactive computer networks to flood your mind with ideas from experts, eccentrics, and visionaries.

If you are looking for a way to bring true love into your life, you may have to learn a lot more about relationships, in general, and take steps to do so. You may have to travel or otherwise go out of your ordinary circle to meet the true love you seek, or to find the right attitude for making your relationship work. It is time to use your wisdom in devising ways to learn more about yourself and your world. By doing so, you will become a more interesting, attractive person, one worldly enough to recognize the traits necessary in one you want to spend your time with.

Affirmation:

I am worthy of respect because I am respectful of all.

Lesson 22. Respect

How deserving of respect you feel, as well as how willing you are to show respect for others, is crucial to your search for true love. To make the most of the energies operating in your life now, you have to ensure that you command respect by cultivating your very best qualities.

Respect and authority are two sides of the same coin. If you are in a relationship you want to improve, you must examine your existing attitudes. Problems with authority can get in the way of your ability to show respect. There may be resentment toward authority that prevents necessary actions from being taken. There may be reluctance to take on the role of an authority because of negative associations with that very necessary role. Beware of those with an unclear understanding of authority and respect, for sometimes they show it as a condescending or downright hostile attitude. Remember to look beyond surface appearances to see the person as he or she really is, for better or worse. If you do not, do not be surprised if you are treated the same way.

Sometimes we must defend the boundaries we must set to protect ourselves from the invasive or inappropriate behavior of others. If we feel undeserving of respect, we won't get it, and we'll have much more work to do later when others go too far. If you would like to bring true love into your life, you must respect yourself and show that same respect for all you meet. If you find it difficult to respect yourself, be aware that the people you respect the most also have these natural feelings of self-doubt. Feelings of inadequacy never leave any of us, but those who come to respect themselves learn to accept themselves as they are.

Lots of disrespect results from cultural egotism and prejudices. Do your best to root out poisonous ideas such as racism, sexism, and ageism in yourself and notice them in others. Equal partners make successful relationships. There is no other way.

Affirmation:

*I am strong and secure.
I stand up for my beliefs,
no matter who they
might disturb.*

Lesson 23. Experiment

How willing you are to champion unpopular, unconventional, and downright eccentric ideas, people, places, and things can be an indicator of the same kind of courage you'll need to bring true love into your life. To make the most of the energies operating in your life, you have to come up with new and different ways of doing things.

It is not easy to rebel against conventional wisdom and bring a much-needed breath of fresh air into your love life. However, it is very rewarding to do so. In addition, to resist taking action against a situation you find intolerable only delays the inevitable time when you will act. Do not let fear of ridicule or the fear of reversing old beliefs and ways of behaving stop you. It is time to discover the latest ideas and unconventional methods for bringing more love into your life.

Now is a good time for exposing yourself and others to unusual viewpoints, theories, and maybe even unusual experiences, too. Think, say, and do what you want without fear of embarrassment, contradiction, or rocking the boat. Avoid censoring yourself or others, and be especially careful of those who would like to censor you, for sometimes you simply must stir things up a bit.

Most of our lives are spent trying to build things up and to make them last. However, the old ways of doing things can become counterproductive. Sometimes instability can lead to inventiveness. Prepare for a time of extremes and expect the unexpected. Be aware that what seems like an accident, mistake, or failure may be a short-lived opportunity for achieving the love you want by an unusual route.

Don't rely on a false sense of security built on the denial of what is really going on. Though this might be a time of rebellion against limitations, precede your actions with a dispassionate, scientific examination of your life as it's currently configured. Be ready for the sorrow and anger that may arise when you fully recognize the negative effects of the status quo. It's even harder to fight established order if you're also fighting your own ego. Don't discard the good aspects of the old life as you root out the bad.

Affirmation:
I am patient.

Lesson 24. Endurance

It is very important for you to be both realistic and patient during the sustained effort needed to bring your desire for love into reality. To make the most of the energies operating in your life, you have to endure the natural obstacles that will arise even if you are doing everything that is humanly and divinely possible. Big things move slowly and sometimes you just have to wait for big things like love. When you are waiting, of course, time seems to pass very slowly.

We often despair when we want things to be different. But remember, there is goodness in things as they are. If you appreciate the here and now, you will find the wait for your Soul Mate easier to endure. Living in this moment will also enable you to stay alert to opportunities you might otherwise miss.

Embrace the discipline of endurance as a spiritual practice only when the goal you want to reach and the circumstances you must experience don't violate your values. You don't have to endure unfair or poor treatment. There is no benefit in enduring a violent or abusive situation.

Though your goal is to attain true love, you must realize that you cannot attain it without also cultivating patience with yourself, others, and with your circumstances. Your goal is contentment rather than constant pleasure or excitement. We can know true contentment when we embrace the present moment and stop struggling to escape insecurity, pain, and doubt.

When you finally attain your love, you will also find a whole new set of things to wait for. Decide now that you will develop the ability to endure without having everything you want immediately. If you do not, success may seem always out of reach, and you will never really enjoy your life.

Endurance, when practiced consciously as a character-building lesson, gives us time for valuable self-reflection. Our life moves at the rate we can deal with. To resist this truth is to invite abrupt and disruptive change.

Affirmation:
I honor all I have done to bring me to where I am in my life today.

Lesson 25. Self-Esteem

A person with good self-esteem is like a positively charged magnet that draws to her the right people and events at just the right time. Low self-esteem makes you vulnerable to anyone who thinks he knows better than you do. Sometimes a person with low self-esteem becomes a belligerent know-it-all to hide the fact that she feels worthless inside. If you or your partner suffer from low self-esteem, you must realize that a real loving relationship will require some adjustment.

The people you bring into your life reflect your feelings about yourself. If you have self-esteem, you will not tolerate shabby treatment from anyone. If you have grave doubts about yourself, you won't respect anyone who praises your good qualities. You will attract those who focus on your weak points because you will think them smart enough to see through your facade, brave enough to confront you, and caring enough to tell you about your foibles. Unscrupulous people use this tactic consciously to manipulate others.

When you decide to improve your life, it's okay to feel uncomfortable or ashamed of the time you might have wasted, the opportunities you missed, and needless suffering you might have put yourself through. The truth is that everything that has happened in your life needed to happen for you to come to where you are now. You are now learning to use your strengths to overcome your weaknesses, the secret of all successful people. You can feel good that you are one of the few people strong enough to face the truth.

Feeling good about ourselves and our accomplishments is not egotism. All too many of us have been conditioned from early childhood not to think highly of ourselves. Parents, siblings, and others often say and do things that lower our feelings of self-worth. We grow up fearing others may think we have a "swelled head." Being afraid to feel good about yourself will generate a whole host of problems in every area of your life. It cannot be stated too often that we need to love ourselves before we can love another person.

We can all feel good about ourselves, for we are all of divine origin. If we are not proud of ourselves, we're not honoring the divine forces that made us, the world we live in, and love itself.

Affirmation:
*I accept my desires as
a pure expression of
my essential self.*

Lesson 26. Desire

Desire drives every relationship and everything we do. All actions begin with a desire for a particular thing to happen. Some quiet time in your sacred space can help you see the difference between what you desire and what others want you to desire. Our desires, however, can be both in our best interests and unreasonable.

Many people do not like themselves and sabotage their best interests because they find some of their desires strange, worrisome, or frightening. Most of our desires are truly ours, but some are the result of our having succumbed to the bombardment of cultural conditioning we all experience from earliest childhood. This same cultural conditioning is why we have trouble accepting our desires and ourselves in the first place. A stunning example of this is a recent study reported in an article about anorexia in *People Magazine*. It indicated young girls are more afraid of being fat than they are of a nuclear war or of their parents dying! That is not something they were born with.

If you are trying to bring a loving relationship into your life, you may be looking for a person with certain desirable qualities. If you examine these desired qualities closely, however, you might see that they're more a result of cultural conditioning than what you actually desire in your heart of hearts. Or the people you're attracting may be responding to signs and behavior you've contrived out of this false conditioning rather than to manifestations of your authentic self. If this is the case, you're going to attract people who will continue to buy into your charade, which will strain your resources and start you looking for an easy exit. Once you get to know someone intimately, you must be very clear with yourself and with her about what you want from her, and what she can expect from you. Work toward what you really want, because if you do, you're going to get it. When you get what you desire, your life will change in many ways, some of which may surprise you. If you're acting out of authentic desires, the new arrangements won't be anything you can't handle.

Affirmation:

*I am content as I experience
the ups and downs of
everyday life from my
spiritual center.*

Lesson 27. Duality

Duality is the central organizing principle of our reality. We cannot know what light is unless we know darkness. We cannot know the meaning of sweet without knowing sour. Applying this teaching to relationships, it follows that we cannot know who we like without also experiencing who we don't like.

Even in a good relationship, there will be annoying disagreements and miscommunications that will take a lot of your precious free time. There is no way to avoid occasionally feeling hurt and depressed on your path to an enchanted relationship. Only if you or your partner find it difficult to recover equilibrium may you have to seek professional counseling.

As we mature, the giddy highs of youthful exuberance and the crushing lows of frustrated expectations become tempered by a new emotion that we have come to call feeling "happy/sad," a version of what Buddhists call "the middle way." In our case, although we are happy to be together as Soul Mates, relatively healthy, and doing what we love for our living creatively each and every day, the sorrows and frustrations from our past and our present efforts are just as real. Repressing or denying the existence of an emotion gives it even more strength. Rather than avoiding everything that makes us sad, we face them squarely as they come and let ourselves experience both joy and sorrow at the same time. Practicing this kind of acceptance and contentment gives us the strong spiritual center that is the goal of all spiritual teachings.

When you think a wrong decision will ruin your life, remember that nothing is ever as good as you think it is going to be and nothing is ever as bad as you think it is going to be. Nothing is as important as your relationship itself, so it's seldom worth worrying and arguing about the less important things.

Consider, too, the option of remaining undecided on a quarrelsome issue. Lots of times you cause fewer problems by not deciding something rather than rushing into a premature decision. It takes courage and wisdom to admit that, for the time being, it is best to decide not to decide. Sometimes, rather than deciding between one person or another in your quest to find your Soul Mate, the wisest course is to keep seeing them both until a decision becomes clear.

Affirmation:
*I shine awareness and
compassion on my past and
on my habitual behavior.*

Lesson 28. The Past

Our pasts and especially our childhoods live on in our memories and affect our daily behavior. Whether you are alone or with someone, you must become more aware of your habits and patterns of behavior. All of our self-limiting habits and attitudes emerged as protective reactions to painful events in our pasts. Whatever you are unconscious of will manifest itself at the worst possible time and in the worst possible way until you deal with it.

The ways we dealt with challenges in the past can be quite inappropriate now. However, it is the nature of habits to rule us unless we first become aware that they are habits, examine the events that gave rise to them, and become aware when we're acting out of habit. Habits can be transformed through patience, awareness, and substituting positive habits like affirmations and visualizations. Remember that your life will improve if you overcome habitual ways of doing things. If both you and your partner each challenge your own outgrown habits, you'll be much better able to create the enchanted relationship you seek. The nature of habits dictates that we are usually unaware of them, so you will probably need a little loving outside help. If you are trying to bring your true love into your life, ask a trusted friend or relative to help you identify habits and attitudes that seem old-fashioned or inauthentic. Getting outside help will also work for those in committed relationships who lack a willing or able partner.

Affirmation:

I allow romance to touch my heart every day.

Lesson 29. Romance

If you are alone but heeding these "Lessons of Light," you *will* attract romantic love soon. Individual passions differ, so anything can happen and often does. Modes of behavior, beliefs, friends and family, and even a place we have lived in for years will look strange and new when seen through loving eyes. Many people, however, become addicted to the intoxication of romance, to those feelings of huge luck and fearlessness.

It is impossible to know if a romance is going to last and this makes it one of the most maddening and the most exciting experiences of our lives. It seems so vastly important and it may very well be!

When romance envelops you, please try to remember that romantic love is only the first step on the path to an enchanted relationship. If you have truly found your other half, the first blush of romance deepens and gets better in ways that you cannot even imagine. Romance feels so good because you get short glimpses into the same intensity that you'll experience with your Soul Mate. The difference is that when you are with your Soul Mate, you'll not have the anxiety and doubt that everyone does in those first romantic days. We can assure you it's a heavenly way to live.

Above all, Soul Mates want to be together. Though it's wonderful when you find him or her, you do risk the tendency to neglect your spiritual growth and your interactions with the world. You can easily get into the state of just wanting to lie in each other's arms all day long and forget about your connections to the world at large. That feeling washed over us when we first started living together and, though it is nice to occasionally just shut out the world and pretend that you two are the world, living that way all the time would be like trying to live on chocolate cake: it can be done, but it is not really that good for you.

Affirmation:
*I enjoy being of service
to those I love.*

Lesson 30. Service

A relationship starts to become serious when both parties want to work with and for each other, either on the relationship or by merging their skills to earn a living. Partners in love can make great partners in business as long as they follow the same "Lessons of Light" in both work and love. In the future, we predict that more and more couples are going to work together. When you work with someone you love, you always want to do your best for him; there is no better incentive to teamwork. You don't waste energy wondering if your partner is all right or if she will be coming home late. All of your energies get channeled into making your business an extension of your relationship. A world of businesses built on a foundation of love would be a truly enchanted place!

Those without partners in jobs they love may find the opportunity to meet someone who shares their interests and passions. It is also possible that if you dislike your work, you might meet someone who shares that passion, sort of like the bond that forms between prisoners. Relationships that come together inside negative situations, however, have to safeguard their dawning affection when the bad job disappears. Unless other attractions, common interests, and ideals are also part of those relationships, they usually vanish along with the unpleasant circumstances.

Sometimes one partner must put his or her own needs second to the other for a time. Soul Mates do this gladly, but if this imbalance goes on too long or if the partner providing service is asked to do things that they are not willing to do, the relationship can founder.

The issue of whether or not to give up work for the sake of your partner, for whatever reason, is a real problem for many people, especially women. Though our marriage is totally fulfilling, substituting marriage for self-fulfillment usually does not work. Marriage rewards you emotionally, but the psychological and material rewards you reap from your own fulfilling work are priceless. However, a career is not something to which you have to completely commit your life. We feel so blessed to have evolved a balanced relationship that works on all levels. You can do it too.

Affirmation:

I pledge my love forever in partnership to you, my beloved Soul Mate.

Lesson 31. Partnership

If you are in an existing relationship, take some quiet time in your sacred space to consider your present partnership in the light of reasonable but uncompromising standards. Of course, no relationship ever attains ultimate perfection. We are lucky that ours stays highly satisfying. It does so partly because we envision an ideal that gives us a goal to work toward. The process of working toward that and other goals together constitutes the essence of a living, breathing partnership.

However, if even the idea of working together on the basic essentials of partnership—mutual trust, honesty, respect, and equality—seems impossible, you may have to confront the fact that your relationship is not a partnership. If this is the case, our "Lessons of Light" and the your own lessons from this pairing will help you to find your enchanted relationship next time.

If you are seeking love in your life, you must be careful not to let your knowledge of what a partnership ought to be interfere with the natural progression of a budding romance. The bonfire of romance burns down to the hearth fire of partnership over time, through patience and hard work. You must wait until you are both totally devoted to each other before you try to make a satisfying, safe, and secure world for yourselves.

Every romance is a celebration, but a committed partnership of loving Soul Mates that proves its strength and value over time justifies the celebration of a whole circle of friends and families because it is truly one of the greatest experiences possible to us as human beings. This celebration of commitment can be an engagement, traditional marriage, or a ritual gathering of the partners' own choosing. There are not enough great partnerships in the world, so they must be celebrated as living examples to inspire us all.

When you are in a true loving partnership, the teachings of the world's great philosophers come alive in a fresh way. Words like love, cherish, caring, patience, trust, and sharing take on a new meaning. We believe it is possible to attain spiritual enlightenment through a loving relationship. Soul Mates do this by seeing the divinity in each other every day.

Affirmation:

I embrace my sexuality as a gift to be shared only with my Soul Mate.

Lesson 32. Sex

Whether you are alone, dating, or have found your Soul Mate, your sexual appetite is just that, yours. How you reveal your sexual preferences, if at all, is an individual matter. However, our sexual urges tear away the mask of anyone who tries to deny them in themselves and in others. If you somehow still reach a non-erotic level of intimacy and commitment with your partner, you may find yourself developing strange compulsions and obsessions that, upon examination, are your Higher Self's way of compelling you to reveal your true self to your Soul Mate, sexually and otherwise.

Almost everyone's sexuality has not escaped the influence of sexual exploitation and repression. Take a frank look at your sexuality and sexual imagination to make sure you are being true to your sex drive and not to someone else's perversion of it.

Today, everyone has to rethink casual sexual relations, which can imperil their lives and the lives of their future sexual partners if they continue to engage in unsafe practices. As long as acquired immune deficiency syndrome (AIDS) threatens, you are wise to delay having sex until you both are certain in head and heart that you are both disease-free and there is a true and potentially lasting bond between you. The reward for this is real sex and real power.

Many who fear commitment are afraid to face a future where they will never have sex with anyone besides their partner. When you really love someone, you want to be with that person as much as possible and in every way. Soul Mate sex is head and shoulders above casual or illicit sex.

Young people especially don't believe that a loving, exclusive relationship can make irrelevant the acquisitive and raging sex drives of "normal" people. They assume us married people repress our desire to have sex with other people in exchange for a pleasant life with regular if boring sex. Staying faithful is not something Soul Mates have to think about. The idea of hurting each other in exchange for—what? Massaging one's ego? Feeling that you still have "it?" To be unfaithful to each other would be a crime against ourselves as well as our love. If the mere encounter with someone else's sexual organs is worth hurting your partner's feelings and risking disease, death, and the ruin of your relationship, then your relationship was not very good in the first place.

Affirmation:

I speak my truth and expect everyone I love to do so, too.

Lesson 33. Truth

Your ability to fill your life with true love depends on your attitude toward telling the truth and on knowing when others are telling the truth to you. You cannot be truthful with another person unless you are first truthful with yourself. Cultivating the habit of telling the truth to yourself enables you to be truthful with others. When you don't deceive yourself or others, you don't have to worry about what you said to whom. Once you examine your own motives for signs of self-deception, you'll be able to consider the motives of others. When you can recognize the half-truths you tell yourself, you'll also be able to recognize the truth when you hear it and know when you are being lied to. This is work that must be done in order to improve an existing relationship or to ensure a positive first meeting with someone who interests you.

It is said that there are no heroes and heroines to act as role models today, but that is incorrect. Soul Mates who give each other the gift of truth are heroines and heroes, indeed. When you have taken the time and done the work of establishing mutual truthfulness in your relationship, you will find you have an incredible amount of time and energy to accomplish many significant things in your life.

It is very important to be open to the truth, whether it hurts or not. The truth really can set you free from illusion and lies. Rather than dismiss your discomfort out of hand, open up your mind to the possibility that you might be hearing the truth, even if it is only true from the point of view of whomever is speaking to you. The humble act of listening shows respect for the person who is trying to speak his truth to you and to the divine within us all.

Affirmation:

I live my life as if my guardian angels are watching me.

Lesson 34. Reputation

Reputation is a very tricky matter because it depends on the words and motives of people outside your relationship. If your good friends are warning you about someone you think may be your Soul Mate, you should give them a fair hearing. However, sometimes jealous or malicious people may try to besmirch your reputation or that of your partner.

It takes time to really get to know someone and vicious rumors can sow doubts that lead to all kinds of difficult situations, especially if you and your partner have not known each other long. If you have been with your partner for a while and especially if you have been working on improving yourself, you will most likely be aware and intuitive enough to separate the truth from any gossip that reaches you. However, if negative reports confirm your own suspicions, it may be wise to initiate some form of investigation to learn the truth before breaking off your relationship. In business, this is called doing your due diligence.

Being diligent also requires you to go within yourself to investigate how much the reputation of those to whom you are attracted affects you. If you are attracted to someone for the possessions, power, or status he or she has instead of who they are inside, this can lead to long-term problems. People who are rich, famous, or powerful may denigrate and take advantage of their "groupies" because they don't respect those who behave that way.

Reputation can also figure into your relationship if you are attracted to moody, brooding, or downright angry people or those with bad reputations. These people can seem to be exciting, powerful, romantic figures guaranteed to keep things from ever becoming dull or boring. However, rather than being sensitive, noble rebels fighting against the status quo, all too many of them are simply acting out their inner rage and are certain to turn it full blast on the people that are closest to them.

A good reputation is a treasure. You cannot undo the past actions that you are now not proud of, but you can make up your mind not to repeat them. The best way to ensure your reputation is to make sure your actions adhere to your highest ideals.

Affirmation:
*I plan for the future with
respect for the unexpected.*

Lesson 35. The Future

The power of the future is the power of the unknown at its most basic and awe-inspiring. We can plan for the future using the most scientific, rational approach, we can consult with "experts" and trend predictors, or we can simply guess what is going to happen, but any plan worthy of the name must expect the unexpected to occur. It always does.

We have all been affected in unforeseen ways by unforeseen events, and this is how things will always be. Unless we can accept this fact of life and have confidence in our ability to deal with whatever situation comes into our lives, we will experience anxiety. Anxiety about the future arises even in the most self-confident people, those who have devoted a lifetime to developing their faith in themselves and a higher power. Having faith in ourselves and in the power of our Higher Self to bring the right experiences into our life at the proper time can help us to cope with this anxiety.

Some people do not give much thought to the future, especially the future of a romantic involvement. They think planning eliminates spontaneity and takes the fun out of things. They do not want to be bothered imagining even the most basic consequences of their actions. They and many other people who engage in self-destructive or risky behavior think the future will take care of itself, and they are right. However, when the future is left to take care of itself, it often does so in an unsettling and unpleasant manner.

The two of us have devoted our lives to studying the phenomena of oracles as a way of improving our decision-making ability. We have learned that each moment contains the potential for an almost infinite number of probable futures. When asked a question about the future, all our different oracles answer you influenced by the scientifically proven principles of chaos theory, enabling the oracle to connect you to the most probable future at the moment you ask your question. This is not fortune-telling, but it can help you make your fortune. Traditionally, oracles have been used as bridges between people and the magic world beyond this one. Each time we consult an oracle we go on a vision quest; we are finding our vision of the future.

Affirmation:
I enjoy being alone.

Lesson 36. Solitude

There are times when it is important for you to put distance, either emotional or physical, between you and your situation or even you and your partner. When you are feeling overly stressed and vulnerable, avoid being overwhelmed by people and events that have no regard for your fragile state. Whether you are trying to bring true love into your life or make an existing relationship better, sometimes you have to keep your distance in order to protect yourself or to make the most of the energies operating in your life.

If you do not put distance between you and those around you, you may find it hard to distinguish between your feelings and theirs. Be around only positive people. Those who are intoxicated, sad, hurt, or angry—including yourself—must either calm themselves or leave. In any event, protect yourself from the insensitivity of others. Isolate yourself from your routine to get in touch with your true feelings. Productive solitude can mean travel, even for a few days, or through the release of a good private cry, which can act like an escape valve for your emotions.

Escape comes in many forms. If you are trying to make an existing relationship better, you may find it beneficial to work on becoming emotionally detached, or you may find it necessary to actually leave the relationship, either for a time or permanently. Sometimes making a strategic withdrawal can give you time to rest and recover your perspective on the situation. You may be surprised at how different things look when you are not stuck in the middle of them. Whether or not you return to the relationship is up to you.

If you are trying to bring love into your life, try going somewhere where you can be completely cut off from your daily routine for a time. Stay out of your own way. If you do not put distance between yourself and your lack of satisfaction with your love life, you may unknowingly sabotage yourself by responding habitually instead of being genuinely present with those around you.

PART III

The Art of Laughter

Chapter Eleven

Humor me

We take our work seriously, but we do not take ourselves seriously. How can we? Our business is a house of cards, literally, since we make a good portion of our income through the production of book and card deck sets. We are doing well and having a great time, laughing every day.

Our religion is creativity. In the presence of a creative impulse, you are filled with a desire to give creative shape to an idea or emotion that arises within you unbidden, or you pray for inspiration and for the ability to become a vehicle for the manifestation of that inspiration. In any case, the creative process is not easy.

Though the artist in our family has never been at a loss for ideas, both of us find the creative process frightening at times, especially the writer in our family who had plenty of obstacles to the development of his self-image as an artist. It is hard to face the challenge of making something the way it deserves to be made; it can drain you physically and emotionally. The judgment that arises out of your internal critic can be more daunting than any other person's criticism and rejection. In fact, we think more creative work has been stopped before it started by people who cannot get past the fear of putting themselves out there by saying, "I am a creative person and this is my work."

What is the antidote to this serious dilemma? Why, humor, of course!

In an artistic life or out of it, if you want to meet your Soul Mate and keep your relationship on track, keep working on your sense of humor. We have found that when we lose our sense of humor, all kinds of troublesome emotions are more than happy to color our worldview with their dark and brooding palette.

Secret: Having a sense of humor is a tremendous asset when it comes to relationships. It is one of the most valuable and attractive features a person can have. If you can keep looking for the humor in your situation, not only will you find it, it can get you through practically any difficult time. It helps you to keep going forward, even in the face of defeat.

Ladies, believe it or not, men highly value women with great senses of humor. Being funny can be more attractive than all of the makeup, clothing, accessories, and scents.

Gentlemen, having a sense of humor is more attractive to women than just about anything else (unless they want to marry a man for some of the wrong reasons). As they say in the movie business, funny is money.

We feel sorry for those men who think this or that possession will impress a woman, when in fact women love men with a sense of humor. Women remember the serious side of life at all times, and they don't forget about death or distract themselves from reality as much as men do. That is why they need to laugh. Being "cute" is big with them.

Here are some cute but true and, we hope, funny stories that will reveal why we cannot take ourselves seriously.

CHAPTER TWELVE

Our Enchanted World—
Welcome to It!

Secret: Make magic, pray, consult the wise. Real magic is when you concentrate on what you love, not what you hate. Believe that there are unseen forces that protect, connect, and sustain us. When you see the hidden connections, the world becomes charged with symbolic meanings. Magic rituals and prayers help us to remember our connection to these unlimited energies that nurture and beckon us to reach our full potential, and that we will do the work necessary to keep that connection clear and unbroken. Prayer is a form of magic in which we seek to ally ourselves with the Divine.

Magic happens and it often happens when you least expect it. Our meeting is a perfect example of that. I, Monte, like to think that although I have not been anywhere near perfect in my thoughts and deeds, I've succeeded to the point where the unseen forces that protect, connect, and sustain us all have helped me to experience a most wonderful life on this plane of existence. These spirit helpers certainly help my spirit, but they often have a strange way of going about it, helping me get myself in and out of a lot of very weird situations.

We have chosen not to have nine-to-five jobs and so we have ninety-five jobs. It's always been that way for both of us. If you think being self-employed or working at home is challenging, try being a freelance artist like Amy. You have to be very secure and have faith in your abilities and in people's ability to recognize them and pay you for them.

In my case, I joke that I just cannot keep a job. The truth is that I have numerous skills, not all of them artistic, but I've tried to make an art of the many different things I've done to make a living. My first job as a teenager was selling Crackerjacks in Prospect Park and then hot dogs at Coney Island, thanks to my father's connections. Like so many of my time, I then became a rock musician, singer, and songwriter. Then, after mending my ways, clearing my mind, and practicing astrology professionally, I became a thirty-one year-old production assistant for Public Broadcasting Station WNET in New York City, driving for three or more hours each way every day. I then went on to become a location scout for commercials and TV shows like *The Equalizer* and graduated to being a Location Manager for feature films like *The Money Pit, A Chorus Line,* and the kung-fu musical comedy *The Last Dragon.* My size and ability to keep the peace on the film's rough-and-tumble locations led to my being hired as the personal bodyguard for actor Michael J. Fox during the making of the movie *The Secret of My Success,* living and working with him 24/7 for three months. The friends and stories I accumulated in my music career and on these jobs, as well as the incredible people that Amy has known because of her fine art career and Hamptons upbringing could and will fill a book someday. However, the unseen forces had other plans for us first and magic happened: we became the world's foremost designers of interactive personal guidance systems and gave birth to The Enchanted World of Amy Zerner and Monte Farber.

Living in our enchanted world has its perks and its quirks. We get to go to all kinds of different and exciting events, including many incredible parties in the Hamptons, New York City, and elsewhere. We also use the parties and other social events to try out our divination systems when they are in development.

Wherever we travel, we read our tarot cards for people when we can. It is our service work. Hardly a day goes by that someone doesn't tell us, "You won't believe it, but that reading you did for me came true!" We're both flattered and exasperated—of course we believe it!

Our *Enchanted Tarot* is not spooky or the work of the Devil, though there is a card by that name—it represents playing the game and wearing the mask when you have to, either in business or relationships. A woman once accosted us on a flight as we were studying our own book and cards to prepare for a lecture in Los Angeles. She told us that she was returning from being baptized in the River Jordan by the Reverend Pat Boone, which sounded wonderfully spiritual to us, though I must confess I wondered if Reverend Boone wore his trademark saddle shoes into the water. She glanced at our work and said, "There are no accidents," something that we also believe. We were feeling comforted that her spirituality was real. She was a nice person, the most telling sign of spirituality. But then she asked us if we knew that tarot cards were the work of the Devil. My answer just popped out: "Lady, if we were doing the Devil's work, we'd be in First Class, not back here in Coach with you!"

On rare occasions, the sudden realization that we make a substantial portion of our income from the sale of tarot cards does make us feel like you do when you climb high on a rickety old ladder and look down. However, we are proud of the quality of our work and how it helps people. To us, our tarot is an executive-decision-making tool, a sacred machine that can capture the possibilities and probabilities of the moment and reflect them back to you for your consideration. Expanding your mind and intuition to interpret your reading develops your decision-making abilities and intuition.

We created our *Instant Tarot Reader* book and card set to offer the ability for anyone with any standard seventy-eight card tarot deck (there are more than two hundred different decks!) to do the same kind of instant readings available on our CD-ROM version of *The Enchanted Tarot*. It is so simple, quick, and fun to do that we were able to get ourselves onto QVC and then the Home Shopping Network (HSN).

We moved over to HSN because our last appearance on QVC was sabotaged by an executive there with a born-again ax to grind against tarot cards. Our first appearance on QVC was at night and we sold more than 1,200 *Instant Tarot Readers* in ten minutes. However, on our second outing, we were given a timeslot of 7:00 A.M., Sunday morning, the time when people are getting ready to go to church. We knew then that the rumor was true and that someone was out to get us thrown off QVC.

Our hostess was a lovely woman who is now one of their top salespeople, but back then she was starting out and drew us as her first product. Talk about a trial by fire! The hosts on the shopping channels are completely and professionally perky and she was one of the perkiest. She insisted on picking a tarot card and we had to agree, though we knew that there was the chance she might get a negative answer that would be broadcast nationally. This was live TV! We would never consider removing any of the negative cards from the deck and sure enough, she drew the Three of Swords, which is called "Sorrow" in our *Instant Tarot Reader* system. Amy sheepishly told her that the cards said she was a bit sad about what she had asked about.

"Great!" she replied, a strangely satisfied customer, and proceeded to ask another question. This time she got the Seven of Pentacles, "Frustration." I broke the news to her this time.

"This is fabulous! I'm having a great time. These would be perfect for a party!" were her rapid-fire responses. We were deeply impressed by her positive attitude and refusal to let negative answers spook her. After all, we have been reading our own cards for almost three decades and have gotten all of the negative cards dozens of times. However, we were concerned that the cards she had drawn turned off our home audience. We could not have been more wrong.

"We have a call!" she announced to our national audience. A disembodied voice that sounded more nervous than I was hesitatingly wafted out over the large and brightly lit stage set.

"I once went to a psychic and she told me that I have no soul," was her opening line. I sprang into action saying, "That is precisely why we have invented *The Instant Tarot Reader*, so that charlatans like that person will not prey on people by telling them lies like that. Everyone has a soul, except perhaps the person who told you that nonsense."

I had no sooner put out that fire than a second call came in, this time from Hawaii.

"I am a Kahuna," was her opening line, which for some reason put worried looks on the faces of our host and our producer.

A Kahuna is a Hawaiian holy person, a shaman of great power, and we were being honored beyond what we would have thought possible on QVC. It just shows you that you never know who is watching.

She went on to say, "I have never been interested in tarot cards before, but yours are so beautiful that I have bought a set." This was all well and good, but she added, "And I can see your auras."

That was a bit too far out for QVC and I decided to lighten things up by replying, "I hope they match our outfits!"

"As a matter of fact, they don't!" she responded, but they cut her off before we could hear about our astral color scheme. By this time we were convinced that no one was going to buy our work, but we were wrong. We sold out, which meant we had sold more than a thousand copies of *The Instant Tarot Reader* in ten minutes, which was great. We then went on to sell thousands on the Home Shopping Network and their website.

Another amusing TV moment occurred when we were on *Good Day New York*, FOX Television's popular morning show. We are regular guests there and do mini tarot readings for phone-in callers. How do we do it? My father always said I walked around in a trance and I suppose he was right because by simply visualizing the situation in question, we are usually able to correctly answer people's questions even if they are not physically present.

One morning, a woman's desperate voice came over the studio loudspeakers. "Will my son ever get out of jail?" she inquired. We looked at the cards and simultaneously said, "No!" There was a pregnant pause as we all wondered if honesty had been the best policy in this case. "Good!" she exclaimed.

The majority of our time away from home is spent in business meetings and giving lectures and workshops on special trips and cruises and at conventions and trade shows dedicated to our various niche markets. They have produced many of the high points of our lives.

We have enjoyed ourselves mightily on our three Intuition Cruises and four Inner Voyage cruises, thanks to Peter and Patricia Einstein. We spend every cruise lecturing, laughing, and getting to meet our ever-widening circle of fans, friends, and fellow authors. We are listing the names of many of the authors we have come to know and respect in the hope that you will also get to know them by including them on your reading list. We have cruised with Richard N. Bolles, James Van Praagh, Shakti Gawain, Larry Dossey, Joan Borrysenko, Ilana Rubenfeld, Paul O'Brien, Gary Zukav and Linda Francis, Susan Miller, Raymond Moody, Dannion Brinkley, Barbara Biziou, Kelly Howell, Caroline Casey, and Yakov Smirnoff.

As you can imagine, spending a week at sea with these brilliant people and our often equally brilliant attendees is a rare gift. Our New Age adventures sometimes range from the sublime to the ridiculous, which we enjoy just as much. These experiences challenge all of our preconceived notions. For example, on one cruise, a conservatively dressed woman's reply to our casual inquiry regarding where she was from was greeted with her equally casual reply, "From the Pleides star group, of course." We know our beliefs can sound just as strange to other people, including many dear friends, so we behave like true skeptics by keeping an open mind and a closed mouth. As the great British naturalist Sir Thomas Huxley said, "I'm too much a skeptic not to believe that anything is possible."

With as many as seven hundred people in our cruise group, we have turned these floating cities into the kind of world we all would like to live in, and not just because while onboard you don't cook and clean up after yourself! If you have a problem on any level, a dozen healers gather around you to work their magic. The degree of kindness, shared wisdom, and sense of community we have enjoyed point the way to the enchanted world available to us all right here and now.

The land-based Prophets Conferences, founded by Robin and Cody Johnson, have taken us to Key West, Santa Fe, and the sacred Mayan sites in the Yucatan jungle. There we have shared the wisdom of many of the most forward thinking individuals of our time. Mayan elder Hunbatz-Men, Greg Braden, Edgar Mitchell, Barbara Marx Hubbard, Kevin Reyerson, and James Twyman, among others, have all inspired us with their wisdom and wit. I have been particularly taken with the astonishing work of pioneering ancient civilizations scholar Zecharia Sitchin, author of the incredible "Twelfth Planet" series, and have been inspired to attend his advanced workshops around the country. Studying with him and Professor Arnold Keyserling of the University of Vienna has had a most profound effect on us.

The International Tarot Congress in Chicago, a biannual event, brings together the writers of the tarot world like Stewart Kaplan, James Wanless, Rachel Pollack, Mary K. Greer, Christine Payne-Towler, and Thalasa, with tarot artists Brian Williams (also an author), Julie Cuccia-Watts, and others.

Also biannual is the United Astrology Congress, which brings astrologers from all over the world to a central location; I cannot say that it brings them together. Astrologers are like rabbis, put two of them in a room and you get three opinions. But we have made friends there, especially with Michael Lutin, astrologer for *Vanity Fair* and *American Way* magazines.

Everyone at UAC wears a name tag that also has his or her astrological Sun, Moon, and Rising Sign on it, which tells any competent astrologer a lot about who they are talking with. We are always disappointed to leave after several days of this wonderful aid to personal interaction and realize that everyone doesn't wear their chart on their "sleeve," so to speak, back in the "real" world.

The semiannual International New Age Trade Shows founded by Susie Hare and held in Denver and Orlando have also proven to be wonderful ways for us to make friends with the people who sell our books, spiritual power tools, and related products. After acting as Master of Ceremonies for their Authors Breakfast, I was "gifted" by a self-proclaimed medical intuitive with the knowledge that I had the worst case of yeast that she had ever encountered, so bad that she could smell me across the cavernous ballroom the second I walked in the door! I was totally taken aback by this uninvited diagnostic overkill. I briefly considered changing colognes. It also was yet another reminder that you should be both a skeptic and a good detective when you are deciding on who to use as a counselor or a healer, intuitive or otherwise. I am robustly healthy and, according to traditional medicine, totally yeast free. But I finally remembered that I drink a lot of Kombucha tea, a fermented beverage made from a pancake-like mushroom and fermentation is usually a by-product of yeast. So I savored that experience as exemplifying the extraordinarily zany experiences that are our daily fare here in the enchanted world.

Even the way we became authors and book packagers is more than a little strange. In 1986, our friend Lori Solensten decided that she was going to publish my *Karma Cards* book and card set. Lori had gotten to know Amy in the 1970s when she was an executive for Tri-Chem, the fabric paint and crafts company for whom Amy did the doodle posters (if you have one, hold on to it—it's worth a lot of money!). Lori had become quite an entrepreneur and her publishing company, Sunstone, was enjoying success publishing the late Dannan Perry's *Essene Book of Days*.

I had given Lori one of the two complete sets of *Karma Cards* that I had formulated on file cards and perfected over the years. I had invented them because, after I quit drugs and the musician's life, I had gone full force into astrology as a profession, reading charts and living and breathing it. Amy and I became the life of so many parties that when we left, they would beg us to stay and say, "I wish you could come up with a way that we could have fun with astrology without you!" I decided to see if I could do it.

The *Karma Cards* are three stacks of twelve cards each, a deck of Planet, Sign, and House cards. When an astrologer reads your chart, they look at where the planets are in order to interpret it. I broke the meanings of the planets, signs, and houses of astrology into sentence fragments that fit together to make six sentences that would answer questions, either what the outcome of a situation would be or what should be done about it. It was one of those simple ideas that has never been done because it was almost impossible to do. There were 10,368 possible sentences that all had to make sense. I did it before I owned a computer, and I truly believe that it rewired my brain and enabled me to go on to invent our other oracles.

Every time we would consult the *Karma Cards,* both my set and Lori's kept advising us, independently, that we should not be publishing *Karma Cards* together, but we did not tell each other, which was almost a big mistake. By the time we got to the booksellers convention in New Orleans that Lori had invited us to, we both admitted it. Lori decided that the she was too small a publisher for such a project. Her professionalism is as great as her friendship.

Amy and I went to the show the next day, undaunted by this turn of events. It is very important to believe in yourself and your work, no matter what setbacks befall you. I walked by a small booth with a copy of *The Book of Runes* mounted on their sign. Amy and I introduced ourselves to the two very nice and very British men, Nick Eddison and Graham Sadd, whose company, Eddison/Sadd Editions, had packaged Ralph Blums' seminal work, *The Book of Runes*, which had already sold several hundred thousand copies and was the first new oracle to be published by a book publisher, Thomas Dunne, who has his own imprint with St. Martin's Press.

I told Nick and Graham that I had an astrology card game that told the future. They immediately asked if they could play it with me. As Amy went down the aisle to see if she could find a publisher interested in doing an art book of her work, they shuffled the cards and silently asked a question. The answer they received was unquestionably and overwhelmingly positive. I asked them what their question had been. To my delight, they replied that they had asked what the outcome would be of their packaging *Karma Cards* for publication and we shook hands. It was as easy as that!

Whereas the music and art businesses had been buildings without doors for us to enter, the publishing industry opened like a flower. An important secret is that when things are right, you do not have to force them. If you find yourself having to force something too much, it is probably not right for you. This is as true in romantic relationships as it is in business.

The flower kept on opening. At the same moment that I was striking a deal with Eddison/Sadd, Amy had walked up to Stuart Kaplan at his U.S. Games booth and shown him slides of her fabric collage tapestries. He was taken with her work and asked her to execute two tapestries of tarot cards as samples for a deck that he would publish. Two potential deals in two minutes of each other! Coincidence? I don't think so. In astrology, the fortunate transits of Jupiter happen every twelve years. If you do the math, you realize that 1986 was twelve years after Amy and I met in 1974 and our good fortune was timed perfectly to the return of Jupiter to the position it was in at the time we first met. It was time for a new twelve-year cycle of growth and good fortune to begin.

Six years later, when Jupiter was halfway around the solar system again and opposing its position on the day we met, an equally important angle in astrology, our hard work and dedication was rewarded again when good fortune smiled upon us with equal flair at another bookseller's convention. Most people know what a Ouija board is. It is a copyrighted rendering of the kind of "talking board" that has existed in many cultures literally for thousands of years. Talking boards are spiritual tools and, unfortunately, the Ouija has too often been sold and used as a toy. It has scared the wits out of a lot of people, and not just young people either.

We thought, "Why should all this ancient wisdom be ignored just because no one is taking the time to see what the ancient sages were really saying?" We had spent much of our lives studying these things, so we thought we'd put what we know into our books.

We wanted to create a talking board system that was prettier, more fun, and easier to use. It would have to be true to our personal goal of helping everyone develop their intuition and decision-making abilities and making ancient wisdom accessible, practical, and useable to all. And very importantly, we wanted to include a comprehensive book that would properly prepare a person to use this very powerful spiritual tool.

In true enchanted world style, we had first been advised to do *The Psychic Circle* by a spirit on a talking board. And we were told to do so fifteen years before we actually did it—before we even dreamed of creating divination systems and writing books!

It was back in 1976 and Amy and I had only known each other for a couple of years. We were enjoying a visit from Lori when Amy mentioned that she had bought a Ouija board in a thrift shop. She had not used a talking board since her teenage years and invited Lori to try it with her.

Being familiar with the power of prayer and ritual, we all held hands and prayed together to surround ourselves with white light, asking that only energies from the highest levels of the world of spirit would come through. And then—nothing.

For what seemed like a long time, we all just sat there, me with my pencil ready to record any information and them with their hands on the board's indicator. Suddenly, the indicator started circling the board and increasing its speed with each turn. We were laughing at the exuberance it displayed, finding it hard to believe that neither one of them was pushing the indicator, when it spelled out: "I am of kin." Even as I write the words now, more than twenty-five years later, I still get the same electric feeling that seeing those words produced in us all that night.

The board proceeded to tell us that the disembodied spiritual essence we were experiencing was a departed relative. Without going into the details of the information given as proof of identity, we received a good deal of material that turned out to be quite important to us all many years later. One example is that during the first session and the sessions that followed, we received the name *Karma Cards* as well as the name and idea for *The Psychic Circle* itself.

After our "kindred" spirit had left, a new energy arrived. The board spelled out: "I am Van Fuld, William Fuld's brother." We all laughed because there, printed at the top of the Ouija board was the name William Fuld, the man who invented the Ouija board and sold it to Parker Brothers, the game manufacturers who had made a lot of their fame and fortune with it.

In the spirit of investigation, which is the best way to approach the use of a talking board, we continued. Well, good old Van really got going. I was keeping the notes of the letters indicated by the talking board's "planchette," the little footed indicator you put your fingers on. Amy and Lori would call out the letters as the marker hovered over them, sometimes with a lot of time between letters, so they didn't know what was being spelled out. They didn't know if anything at all was being spelled out, for that matter!

My eyes widened with surprise as I jotted down the letters, broke them up into words and saw what "Van Fuld" was saying to us on the talking board: "He stole the Ouija board idea from me and now I am going to give you an idea!"

Then the marker started zipping around so fast that everyone could figure out the words being spelled out: "Psychic Circle . . . circle is infinite . . . try to make PC for everyone . . . one heaven for everyone . . . 18 inches diameter in square . . . not the size of a place-mat . . . there should be maybe planets, symbols, and signs . . . see nature—sea (water), and nature (earth)—sky (air) . . . something like a tweeter [the Magical Message Indicator of our *Psychic Circle* looks like a small clear plastic high frequency speaker] . . . six levels . . . represents the cosmos . . . be patient."

We were patient, all right. We were so patient that we totally forgot about that session for fifteen years. And then our masterful astrologer, Leor Warner, whom we had never told about the session because, after all, we had forgotten it, said to us in our semiannual reading, "It's time for you to do that round talking board." It stunned us to have him remind us of something we had never told anyone—so much so that we took it as a sign that we had an idea whose time had come.

The problem—there is *always* a problem—was that we only had a couple of days to prepare before taking off for the bookseller's annual convention, BEA, in Anaheim to promote *Goddess Guide Me,* our first Goddess project from Simon and Schuster. Usually, you have to have a fairly detailed proposal—an outline with a chapter, a draft, a one-page description—something! However, we had our ever-present spirit of adventure, a name for the project given to us by the disembodied and vengeful Van Fuld, faith that we could sell this project on the idea alone, and a track record of selling our products.

What ended up being our lucky charm came from a plastics store on Canal Street in New York City. We were there a few days before our trip to order more of the plastic rods that Amy sometimes uses to support her smaller tapestries in the manner of a scroll. We had been trying to decide on the design for our very own planchette for *The Psychic Circle* and there it was, a small, thin, clear plastic piece sitting in a pile of ten-cent odds and ends looking like a transparent hockey puck. Amy has eagle eyes and she picked it up triumphantly exclaiming, "This is it! This is the Psychic Circle!" I was excited, too, but the salesman was not impressed, though he did give it to us for free with our order.

So we went to the convention and made the rounds of the publishers we had already worked with. We had no proposal so we just told all of them that we were going to package *The Psychic Circle,* a round Ouija board that was a thousand times easier and better than that old chestnut. They all wanted it, but it was Simon & Schuster who agreed to let us manufacture the largest quantity for the most reasonable price and in October of 1993, *The Psychic Circle* was published.

We've heard from thousands of people who've used our *Psychic Circle* to contact loved ones who have crossed over, find missing objects, and change their lives for the better. It has became one of our "evergreen" best-sellers, the kind of book publishers and packagers love because it sells thousands of copies each and every year. Equally important is that when I sneak in for a peek at the talking board chat rooms on the Internet, more and more of them are now called "Ouija/Psychic Circle." We're starting to win back the good reputation of talking boards. Now, how many people can say that with a straight face?

Six years later, in 1999, our Jupiter cycle struck again and we created and packaged *The Pathfinder Talking Board* for Tuttle Publishing's Journey Editions imprint. I'm sure you won't bat an eyelash when I tell you that it was *The Psychic Circle* who gave us the idea.

The Pathfinder uses the metaphor of the "Vision Quest" taken by the world's shamans. During a Vision Quest, these most powerful of human beings, like Mayan elder Hunbatz Men, go off by themselves to fast and endure terrible privations, in order to prepare themselves to face the ultimate enemy—fear. Their goal is to encounter themselves completely and by facing and befriending their fears, they come back to their tribes as fully integrated humans, better able to serve the spiritual needs of their people. Amy and I are very aware that many Native Americans are quite sensitive about those not born into their culture doing projects based on it, so I asked Hunbatz for his blessing before *The Pathfinder* was published and he gave it to me saying, "We have to make thousands of shamans now. We are entering sacred times."

In a very real way, *Love, Light, and Laughter* is the story of our Vision Quest. Although the stories I've told you about these four of our more than fifteen publishing successes are completely true, you can be certain that not everything about these projects has gone as smoothly for us in our career and personal lives. You can be equally certain that each and every day of our enchanted lives contains at least one reminder to us that we are living a wonderful dream surrounded by humorous friends on both sides of the curtain that divides our world and the world of our departed friends and spirit guides. If you don't believe me, ask *The Psychic Circle*!

MONTE: AMY'S FORTIETH BIRTHDAY, OR WHY HUSBANDS SHOULD ALWAYS BE FUNNY

We're about to go sappy on you, with good reason. It's important to note important birthdays and other anniversaries. Doing only that—and not connecting with each other on an everyday basis—will not, however, an enchanted relationship make. But if we don't mark these occasions we risk losing our impetus to celebrate the everyday.

We are now going to share two very important occasions we've marked in our relationship—and a few of the funny lessons we learned from them.

Much is made of turning forty and with good reason. As Rousseau said, "Forty is the old age of youth and fifty is the youth of old age." When you are forty you are definitely not old, but you are just as definitely not young, either. Calling it the midlife crisis presupposes that you are going to be smart and lucky enough to live to be eighty, but when you hit forty you are not so sure the odds or gods are on your side. For those brave enough to look back on their life to judge how closely their accomplishments match the goals of their youth, it is a sobering time. For those whose last sober thought was in their early teens, it is a critical make-or-break time.

From an astrological standpoint, the midlife crisis, is associated with Uranus, and not just because most men who turn forty start acting like a**holes. Forty represents the time when the planet Uranus, the butt of most astrological humor (okay, I'll stop it, but this is very appropriate Uranian behavior!), has come halfway around the solar system from where it was the moment you were born. This is the time of the "Uranus opposition," in astro-logical jargon.

Uranus, takes approximately eighty years to go around the solar system, give or take a few, so the Uranus opposition could hit you a couple of years earlier or later, depending on the date you were born. So what, you might well ask? Well, it is more than worth the ten minutes it takes to find out just when in your life Uranus is going to hit you. I would recommend giving yourself a reading with a good astrologer for your thirty-sixth birthday. Forewarned is forearmed. The energies of Uranus are not something you want to fool around with.

Actually, you *should* fool around, not with Uranus, but with your life, for that is what Uranus governs, especially when you are forty. Uranus symbol-izes the energies in your psyche and in your life that want to keep you from being bored and being boring. It wants you to make your life a statement of your special originality and, if you have done so, then the influence of Uranus will help you enjoy the rewards of all the hard work of resisting your fears about becoming yourself fully and avoiding conforming to other people's expectations. The incredible energy you expend comes back to you in that particularly wild and crazy Uranian form of startling surprises, unexpected good times and good fortune, and exciting events you never dreamed could happen. Even at their best, the "birthday gifts" Uranus gives you for your fortieth birthday invariably disrupt the status quo of your life, but ultimately for your greater good and highest joy, though you might not think so at the time.

The trouble with the Uranus opposition comes if you haven't made your life a statement of your special originality. In that case, all the energy you have put into resisting becoming yourself fully and in squeezing yourself into other people's expectations will explode into your life, usually at the worst possible time and in the most disruptive way imaginable. It's a time when people quit their jobs, start associating romantically with much younger, much older or very different people, take up activities that leave everyone around them scratching their heads in fear and disbelief, and make car and motorcycle salespeople's days by buying fast machines. The color? "Midlife Crisis Red," of course. Think about some of your friends and how they have handled turning forty. Enough said!

How do you deal with this eccentric Santa Claus of a planet that knows if you've been wacky or straight? At the very least, do something different, wild, and fun. If you do not, Uranus is more than willing to help you, though not in any way that you would ask for unless given truth serum. In the long run, it's easier to make the effort to bring a breath of fresh air and excitement into your life than to watch the doors and windows of your nicely packaged existence kicked in and blown out by forces beyond your control.

Amy and I have worked full time to make our life a work of art and our art a work of life, but we knew that the forces of Uranus needed acknowledgment at forty. So I decided to make Amy's fortieth birthday party a surprise.

Most husbands have a problem with pulling off a surprise party, but it was harder for me because we live and work together all the time, and we are both psychic. Normally, I love this, but it does make throwing a surprise party a challenge. Challenges like that are preferable to picking up the pieces after an unacknowledged Uranus give you its birthday gift, so I applied a couple of the secrets of making magic to surprise my love and give Uranus its due at the same time.

My mind was primed for designing this "game" of surprise. I had already invented the systems for my first and third divination systems, *Karma Cards* and *The Alchemist*, and written the text for *The Enchanted Tarot* book, explaining the intricacies of the tarot and what I saw in the seventy-eight incredible fabric collage tapestries that Amy created for our very own tarot deck. My mind had been rewired, and I had confidence that my intuition would guide me to do this just right.

Our first rule of magic is usually, "pee first," but this was going to be a month-long process, not a ceremony of normal duration, and so I moved on to the second rule of magic: keep it secret. The Book of Tao says, "One who overcomes others is great. One who overcomes her or himself is greatest." One meaning of this is that when you resist the urge to blab, I mean to give voice to your intention, you can harness that power to work your will on your reality. So the best way to keep a secret or to work a magical plan is to tell no one you are doing it. *No one.*

Amy's dear mother, Jessie, never forgave me for not letting her in on my surprise, but I knew that there was no way that anyone could keep this secret: I was going to surprise Amy with a trip to Paris! In the past, I had surprised her in little ways, with gifts like a crystal ball ring she had admired stuffed into the business end of an elaborately wrapped pogo stick, but this "Paris Package" had to be the mother of all surprises.

When I was younger, I had read a brilliant line of strategy in one of G. K. Chesterton's Father Brown mysteries that has stayed with me my whole life. "Where do you hide a leaf? In the forest!" Father Brown was referring to a murderous general who had concocted a whole battle's worth of bodies to hide his crime, the body of his wife's lover. I knew that if I were going to give Amy a surprise gift, then I would have to hide it in a bunch of other gifts.

I told her that I was throwing her a party, which distracted her completely. Normally, if we are going to be traveling, a suitcase worth of my clothes will mysteriously disappear a month before departure; she packs that far in advance! Amy is the hardest working person I know or have ever heard of and she never, ever leaves anything to the last minute, like some people I know, me included.

One of the hardest things about making this trip come off was going behind Amy's back and undoing all the appointments she had made for the five days we were going to be in Paris. The people I called must have thought I was crazier than I am because of the strange excuses I made up, designed to cancel her appointment without telling them the truth or giving them a reason to call back.

I had to tell the travel agent what I was doing to prevent her from calling our house, but this turned out to be the best thing I could have imagined (thank you, Uranus!). The travel agent thought my surprise trip for my wife was the most romantic thing she had ever heard of and told the Intercontinental Hotel in Paris what I was doing. This was March of 1991 and just after the Gulf War. There had not been the usual crush of Americans or any other tourists in Paris for quite a while because of fears of retaliatory terrorism, and so when we got to the hotel, I was delighted to find out that the hotel management had given us an enormous suite at no extra charge! Most of our pictures of the trip were taken in and of that suite, though we did venture out a few times.

The day of the party arrived, and I was more than a little nervous. I had almost everything ready, except I hadn't packed Amy's suitcase. Amy is incredibly intuitive, so I practically had to forget what was going to happen to avoid early psychic detection. I kept coming up with things for her to do that kept her out of our bedroom so I could surreptitiously pack the bare essentials, which are considerable for people like us who don't know the meaning of packing light. The good news was that I had decided not to take any of her clothes and to make the trip a shopping spree at the Galleries Lafayette, the epitome of the chic Parisian department store.

This was obviously going to be an expensive trip, but sometimes you have to take a chance that unexpected benefits will come from extending yourself for a great cause. This was one of those times and certainly one of those causes. Amy and I had taken a trip to Paris once before, in 1985, after I had worked on the very funny feature film *The Money Pit*, starring Tom Hanks and Shelly Long, for five months, living in that Locust Valley mansion and only seeing Amy on the weekends and when she could get away to stay with me during the week. We had done Rome, Milan, Venice, Vienna, and Paris in three weeks and by the time we got to Paris, we were broke. Paris is not a city in which to be broke, and I wanted this time to be different.

The thirty-five guests arrived on time for our Sunday luncheon, the early schedule dictated by Air France's departure schedule. Did I mention that I had prepared most of the food, too? A far as Amy was concerned, that was a wonderful and thoughtful gift in itself, and it totally derailed any suspicions.

Our friends were all having a great time, unaware of what would happen next. I was doing my best not to fold under the pressure and be my usual gregarious self as host. The only time I almost lost my cool was while I was packing Amy's toiletries and heard her coming down the hall. I ran outside the door with nervous sweat on my fevered brow. She couldn't understand why I was barring her from the bedroom she has slept in since she was sixteen years old and so I told as much of the truth as I could—she couldn't come in because I was wrapping her present! She gave me a quizzical look, but she went back downstairs to the party, and all was right with the world.

They were bringing in the carrot birthday cake from Provisions, the Sag Harbor health food store, when I found her. I said I wanted to give her her present right then and there. I pulled a little black box from my pocket. As she opened it, her beautiful smile froze a bit and was replaced by a look that said, "What the—?" as she fished out a cheap, gold-plated pin that said "Paris" and had a miniature Eiffel Tower dangling from it. That's when I lowered the boom.

"Your birthday present is that a limousine is coming in twenty minutes to take us to the airport and we're going to Paris!" I exclaimed in a voice that penetrated the farthest reaches of her studio and the ears of our assembled friends. I will be forever grateful to our nephew, Rune Lind, for capturing on videotape the blood draining from Amy's face like the mercury in a thermometer plunged into ice water as she realized that I was not joking.

Of course, as any woman reading this could predict, Amy went upstairs with a few friends, including Linda Alpern, a registered nurse who could have helped Amy in case of birthday surprise shock, and repacked the suitcase, but only to include a few items of clothing (yes, I had even packed the Tampax!). I stayed downstairs and made sure that the first thing I did was apologize to Jessie for keeping my secret from her. My mission then was to thank everyone for coming and to assure them that the party was supposed to keep going even after we departed, which it did for several hours, I'm told.

The long stretch limo eased itself into our driveway to the delight of the neighborhood kids who acted like it was the Space Shuttle landing. After everyone from the party had climbed in and played celebrity, Amy and I made our final good-byes to the revelers ready to see us off.

Thanks to our friend Melinda, we actually got a backstage and underground tour of the Paris Opera, the very building that Amy had chosen to picture on her image for "The Tower" card of her *Enchanted Tarot*. The Tower is the tarot card most resembling the astrological symbolism of the planet Uranus. When it comes up in a reading, you know that revolution is in the air and something that you have depended upon for a long time and possibly taken for granted is not going to be there for you the same way. It has taken on new meaning for all students of tarot after the horrendous terrorist attacks of September 11th, 2001, the date some astrologers are now using to mark the beginning of the Age of Aquarius, an epoch and sign ruled by Uranus.

Our luck was running over! I had somehow managed to pull off a total surprise, and Amy was delighted, after she stopped being a little play-mad at me for giving her the shock of her life. We both could hardly believe what was happening to us. Here it was, the day after her fortieth birthday party in her studio in East Hampton, Long Island, New York, and now we were walking hand in hand gazing at the indescribably beautiful Eiffel Tower before we rode its angled elevators up to the very top. We were completely disoriented, completely excited, and completely in love. Uranus was satisfied and so were we.

CHAPTER THIRTEEN

The Perfect 22nd/25th Anniversary to a Perfect Wedding

I f you are already married, in fact, especially if you are already married, the creation of an amazing anniversary ceremony is one of the best ways to reinvigorate your marriage. Not only is a renewal ceremony fun, it is a quintessential act of religion, a word that means, "to bind together again."

Like our wedding, the party we threw for our 22nd/25th anniversary was a good one, though it started off resembling the Ten Plagues on the Exodus from Egypt. It began on a Sunday morning, June 11th, 2000, and we planned a midafternoon garden party at our home. We were throwing it to celebrate the 22nd anniversary of our wedding and the 25th anniversary of our living together.

It was a day of great joy and challenge, maybe not as bad as the plagues of Egypt, but beset with the Y2K-in-the-Hamptons kind of plagues (remember Y2K, the millennium computer glitch caused by the computers supposedly being unable to recognize "00" for the year 2000?). We realized immediately that these weren't wars or natural catastrophes, and we did our best to laugh our way through them, though we didn't always succeed!

Traffic was the first plague. The Long Island Expressway funnels drivers from New York City out to the Hamptons, but that weekend it had been closed all the way back in the borough of Queens to repair an overhead train bridge. That bridge must have been ready to crumble any minute if they were willing to seriously annoy a couple of hundred thousand people on their way to summer fun. Many of them, including many of our invited guests, got so sick of being slowly detoured to death on the unfamiliar streets of Queens for four hours that they turned around and went back to Manhattan. Who could blame them?

Traffic didn't daunt our two houseguests, my sister, Karen, and our dear friend Dan Romer, who came out to see us the day before via the very dependable Hampton Jitney bus service. The morning of the party the two of them were helping Amy figure out how to change our party from a garden party to an indoor party on the fly as the second plague, Trial by Fire, befell us.

We decided to move the party out of our little Garden of Eden and into Amy's expansive studio, because the day was promising to be one of the hottest and most humid June 11ths on record. The weather forecasters generated our apprehension by predicting rain for our party time right up until that morning, but then, as if by alchemy, the threat of rain turned into *heat*! Either way, we could no longer count on having more than a hundred people in the garden. (Of course, this was before we knew about Plague of Traffic, which would reduce our party's numbers.) But those were merely the warmups, the prelude to the symphony of real challenges.

The Plague of Explosion, number three, and the Plague of Flying Projectiles, number four, happened next. Amy came downstairs that morning to find that one of five big glass bottles of Kombucha tea (a fermented beverage that I buy by the case and drink for its health benefits and refreshing, yeasty taste) that had been stored the way we always had on the cool tile floor of our kitchen pantry, had burst during the night. There was broken glass and vinegary smelling liquid waiting for her to clean up. While cleaning it up with our cat standing next to her "helping," a second bottle exploded! It sent glass flying all around Amy and our now much-missed Kit-Kat and it is a *miracle* of the first order that Amy and Kit-Kat were not blinded or injured by the glass shards. I will be forever grateful to whatever guardian spirits—probably Ma—accomplished that miracle, for I would have hated myself forever if my stupid beverage had blinded my beloved Amy (or Kit-Kat, who was a sweetheart!).

I came downstairs to the disaster area. I vowed to accept any mission that might redeem me for endangering Amy and Kit-Kat. It was apparent that my mission impossible was to remove the other three bottles before they, too, exploded, as their fermentation inside this particular batch of Kombucha was obviously going like an out-of-control nuclear reaction. But before I found and donned my Eddie Bauer "bomb-disposal gear," I went down to our basement to see if the Kombucha liquid had leaked through onto the basement ceiling and floor.

I was confronted by Y2K-in-the-Hamptons biblical plague number five: Flood. More than two inches of water covered our entire basement floor! The toilet in Amy's studio had broken and the water had run all night (while I was playing rock-and-roll with friends at a local restaurant) and backed up our cesspool, big time. So, grabbing my trusty submersible pump (for prior, less millennial floods), I hooked up my new Martha Stewart garden hose from K-Mart and started pumping the water out of the basement and onto the lawn on the other side of Amy's studio, away from our garden. So, in the ninety-degree heat and tropical humidity, I prepared to do battle with the three remaining Kombucha tea bombs. I pulled on my black Balaclava head mask, donned my trusty black Eddie Bauer down parka, pulled up its down-filled hood and neck flap, and shoved on my thick suede Silvercup Studios ball cap and thick suede gloves, black in color just like the rest of my outfit. The two *pieces de resistance:* my shooting goggles, which I had somehow inherited from our friend Dan's father, a big game hunter, and a padded seat cushion from one of our lawn chairs, which now dangled around my neck like a long baseball umpire's body protector. I looked like a member of Russia's Black Berets special forces unit, ready to play catcher in his first baseball game. I have pictures, but because everything was black, they really don't do it justice. I'll wear it some day for Halloween if it's cold enough.

Sweating like a pig and scared silly that I was going to lose a finger or two, I gingerly opened our pantry door and even more gingerly removed the three bottles, one at a time, and placed them into a couple of insulated plastic blue and white coolers we had bought for the party. I later wrote to Coleman to tell them what nifty bomb disposal cases they make!

I transported the coolers outside, and no sooner had I put them down than two more of the bottles went off! Strangely I couldn't explode the last bottle no matter what I did and I tried as hard as I could. Here comes plague number six. I went to put the glass from the exploded bottles in an old plastic trash can behind our shed, and I noticed that a squirrel had bitten a four-inch hole through its lid. When I removed the lid, I found a puddle of water and a thriving colony of mosquitoes! Holy West Nile Virus, Batman! At this time, the whole metropolitan area was being sprayed from the sky with chemicals designed to kill mosquitoes that might carry the potentially lethal West Nile Virus. I slammed the lid back on, taped up the hole with duct tape, and reopened it a minute later to dump in a small bottle of concentrated organic pesticide and the remains of a spray can of "Hornet and Wasp" spray that I had bought for a previous natural disaster.

Right on schedule, the never-on-Sunday emergency cesspool pumping behemoth truck arrived, pledging to rescue us, at double the normal price, of course. I had spent my every off moment, both of them that morning, going through the phone book of 24/7 cesspool pumpers and being told that they either wouldn't go to East Hampton or they were totally booked that day. Now I had a house where no one could flush a toilet or wash her face or take a shower or use any water—and we had a veritable parade of 100 guests and fifty gallons of expensive liquids and carloads of delicious food for them arriving in two hours!

While I had been going through the phone book, I could hear Amy and Dan and Karen marching around our house, decorating and turning Amy's studio into an exquisite indoor bar and grill. Amy's studio is literally the size of a house and has a second story for storage that does not run the full length of the building. But now the ministering Angels of Poop and their pump truck had arrived, and we were saved, sort of. They had to get their six-inches-in-diameter vacuum hose, which bucks and kicks like a Brahma bull as the liquid rushes through it, through my garden to get to the cesspool. Rising to this creative challenge, I saw that we could use our brand-new lawn chairs to protect the plants we had worked so hard to raise. I really should write to Martha Stewart, who has two houses here in East Hampton, and tell her that her lawn chairs and their cushions are as versatile in their uses as they are attractive.

However, at the time, my mind and my nose were both definitely not concerned with how attractive things looked, but with how disgusting this pump hose that was soon to be bucking in my arms looked and smelled. I am a hands-on kind of guy, and in order to protect my beloved garden, I was determined to stay there every second and hold the hose with the workers so there would be no deaths in my plant family. This was a garden party, after all, and I had spent a small fortune and lots of time on purple flowers and making everything just so.

So, in the 90-plus-degree heat, they opened the cesspool, pumped out two thousand gallons of unmentionable materials, and left, knocking a couple of low-hanging branches off our dogwood tree for good measure. But I didn't care, now our guests would be able to use the bathrooms. It was a good thing. Now I could return our cars to our driveway and the flushing, showering, and primping could begin!

Meanwhile, plague number seven, Power Outages, was going on in the house, and I didn't even know it. While I was fighting and struggling with the giant throbbing pump-out hose outside in the heat, our window air conditioners were cranking. The big AC unit in the living room kept tripping the circuit breakers and darkening the house, before I managed to figure out that the overload was caused by my computer's backup uninterruptible power supply. But before I fixed it, it became just as hot inside as outside, and the caterers were giving us quizzical looks as they scurried about preparing for what they must have thought was an impending disaster for one hundred. Another round of showering became necessary to wash off our nervous sweat. But by then the AC returned, and we saw that it was good.

Never one to be left out, our calico Muse, Kit-Kat, waited until 2:45 to add her two cents by peeing on our hot bluestone patio, exactly where all of our guests would be walking in fifteen minute. So, in my party clothes, I grabbed my trusty garden hose one more time for a patio wetdown and, with the submersible pump pumping out our basement and people calling for directions, the party started promptly at 3:00 P.M.

That is when the eighth plague of 110, befell us: 110 guests in 110-degree heat in Amy's studio whose air conditioner is 110 years old. Friends, their houseguests, and friends of their houseguests started arriving. It had become like Woodstock after the gates had been knocked down. Come on in—the more the merrier! Actually, the rest was fun. We are so used to having a lot going on and having to take care of it ourselves that we were easily able to forget the prior mishaps and concentrate on being host and hostess—so that no one knew what we had just been through.

Precisely at 6:00 P.M., the scheduled end of the party, the skies opened up with a display of plagues numbers nine, ten, and eleven, Torrential Rain, Deafening Thunder, and Lightning, all of which almost put our lights out. In fact, the next day, the phone and electric company trucks moved like an invading army through East Hampton repairing the many downed lines.

Dan made the whole thing even more hilarious when he started making a mock Hamptons gossip report on our party, exclaiming to his sister, "Amy and Monte had the greatest party! They did a Swamp Theme and they had a river in their basement and breeding mosquitoes and exploding swamp gases and thunder and lightning and they even had a Swamp Thing dressed all in black with swamp sweat pouring off him! It was simply fabulous!"

The best part of all this is that neither Amy nor I ever lost our cool. Instead we along with Karen and Dan and laughed off our fear and apprehension.

Secret: Cultivate contentment in all circumstances. Self-doubt is the most daunting of obstacles that inhibit us on our quest for enlightenment. We can know true contentment when we embrace the present and stop struggling to escape insecurity, pain, and doubt.

Amy hardly ever loses her temper. If fact, she is the most patient person that I know, even more amazing because she is in all other ways true to her sign of

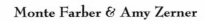

Aries, which is not known for conferring patience. For me, the less temperate Aquarius, it was kind of graduation day. The first time I had realized that spirituality was working for me was when I realized that I was not getting upset in traffic. Instead, I could see everyone as in the same "boat" or car as me, as fully capable of making a mistake and as in need of forgiveness. I love bumper stickers and this spiritual truth was beautifully contained in the one that says "Caution: I drive as badly as you do." But me, laughing through the Eleven Plagues? Well, let me tell you—that was graduation!

> **Secret: Be playful and have fun.** Encourage a sense of adventure. Try to maintain a positive, open attitude even when things don't appear to be going the way you want. Much of the art of living is dealing with the unexpected. See with the eyes of a child. Enjoy yourself and celebrate.

CHAPTER FOURTEEN

Life Is But a Dream

O kay. You have almost finished our book and you deserve to know the truth. Now we know we can trust you with our final secret. How did we really meet? Did we really meet at the filming of a porno movie? Actually, that's not quite true. Sure, we did meet in the flesh for the first time at the filming of a porno movie, but we first met in a dream, a prophetic dream.

Like love, light, and laughter, our dreams, myths, fairy tales, and even nursery rhymes are powerful forces in our lives and essential to our spiritual and emotional development. There is great spiritual wisdom in the nursery rhyme lyric, "Row, row, row your boat gently down the stream. Merrily, merrily, merrily, merrily, life is but a dream." If the purpose of life is to be happy, to be merry, then this wonderful rhyme teaches us how that can best be accomplished: by "rowing gently," not upsetting yourself or other people as you do your best to navigate the river of the Land of Our Dreams.

There is nothing in our lives more magical yet more common to all of us than this land where each of us spends a third of our life. Each night our Higher Self lovingly welcomes us home to this invisible yet omnipresent place where our waking mind's thoughts and our heart's desires are symbolically materialized along with our past, present, and sometimes our future so we may be instructed, nurtured, healed, and sent back to the other side of the landscape of our soul to try and work our will in a land where time and space rule.

MONTE: HOW I DREAMED UP AMY

The happy part of my life really did start because of a dream, a prophetic dream.

I often have prophetic dreams. They warn me of upcoming events or give me an opportunity to practice how I'm going to handle a particular situation. And my first prophetic dream was really my best, for that is where I first "met" my gorgeous future wife, Soul Mate, and artistic collaborator.

It is still vivid in my mind. I was fourteen years old and enjoying a boys-only sleepover, just me and my recently divorced father.

Though my hormones were raging against the apparent uselessness of my incipient manhood, on this steamy summer evening I lay sleeping, tossing, and turning in the grip of a recurring nightmare that had plagued me since childhood. In the dream, all the poor, trapped animals had escaped from the Prospect Park Zoo, where my father had often worked the graveyard shift, midnight until 8:00 A.M. A crowd of gigantic lions and tigers and rhinos and giraffes and elephants—especially the elephants—were kicking up a cloud of dust as they made their way menacingly toward my mother, Karen, and me. The numbing fear I felt and the dust cloud I saw in my prophetic dream resembled what we all experienced while watching video images of the towering cloud of dust produced by the awful collapse of the twin World Trade towers.

But back in 1964 and in my teenage dream, I was a little boy, as I was when I first started having this recurring nightmare. Karen and I were playing in the grass in front of one of the hundreds of concrete and wooden slat benches that ringed the grassy forty acres of the Prospect Park Parade Grounds, sort of like an African savannah with nothing but ringside seats.

In my dream, as the rioting animals got nearer, my mother knew exactly what to do. In my recurring dream she was a tower of strength in the face of this animal jail break, and she took our little hands and helped us across Caton Avenue into the illogical safety of our downstairs tenement hallway. We entered the faux-finish brown marble hallway and turned around to slam the half-glass door shut just before the elephants marched slowly but ominously by our hiding place, their trunks holding each other's tails, like in the circus.

Suddenly a new character burst into my recurring animal dream like breaking news. A beautiful, sexy girl with purple hair (!) sat in front of me while I massaged her lovely neck and shoulders. Keep in mind that the sexual revolution was a few years away! I realize that this dream is tame compared to the dreams that kids must have nowadays, given the bump-and-grind strip shows that music videos, movies, and even TV commercials have become. However, this was big stuff for a fourteen-year-old boy in 1964, a boy who was worried that he would never find a girl who thought him anywhere nearly as attractive as the lucky bad boys (who promptly defamed the girls behind their halter-topped backs if they so much as kissed them).

What made my dream of this nameless woman even more amazing was that I actually felt the indescribable feeling of being in love with her! It was a harbinger of the total and complete love that is my present daily experience. I have come to believe that right there in the middle of my sad and lonely adolescent confusion, my dream energized and purified me for the lean years to come; I knew beyond a doubt that this woman loved and trusted me totally, too.

Before I awoke, I saw myself turning off a main road and going up a hill with the sun shining through the trees, after which I made the peculiar turn-within-a-turn that completes what I now know as the end of the road to the home that she and I have shared since 1975. I often think of this dream when I drive up that hill on a sunny East Hampton day, half expecting to see my fourteen-year-old dream body hovering in the trees. After I woke up, I was in agony! I tried with all my might to go back to sleep and to feel that incredible feeling of pure love but, of course, I couldn't. I tried everything I could think of, even asphyxiating myself, to no avail. I thought I felt a bit of the love, but only as a fading distant echo of the feeling in the dream.

Even then, I instinctively knew that love is meant to be shared. I went into the tiny kitchen and startled my father out of his usual slow reading of the newspaper. I assured his questioning blue-gray cop's eyes that nothing was wrong and excitedly announced that I had just seen the woman I would love and marry in a dream. Solemnly, my father put down his paper, looked at me with a pitying gaze, and said in his best Brooklyn tough-guy voice, "What do *you* know about love?"

A parent who speaks without thinking can turn a child's prophetic dream into a pathetic one. However, I fell back on my cultivated ability to resist the tendency to believe a word he or anyone said, a gift of Grace that had enabled me to survive my earlier childhood. I had seen psychology-influenced television shows where people blamed their parents' influence for everything from rude behavior to murder, and I had determined at an early age that, though I did not know the answer to that most scary of questions, that is what was I going to be when I grew up, I knew I was not going to be a cliché.

My first foray into prophecy got a lousy reception, and I might not have known too much about love then while awake, but since 1975, Amy, who *does* have purple hair, and I have lived and loved together and built the kind of true love and mutually supportive partnership most people only dream about.

The Secrets: The ABCs of Love, Light, and Laughter

A *Appreciate all the good things in life.* Show your love. Show you care. Passion and compassion are what make you attractive. If you would enjoy the passion of love, you must act first with passion. Men are willing to go through a lot to earn the appreciation of their true love, and women, as the keepers of the sacred flame of life, desire to be given the respect they deserve. If you demonstrate your mutual appreciation, true love will deepen and last a very long time.

B *Be playful and have fun.* Encourage a sense of adventure. Try to maintain a positive, open attitude even when things don't appear to be going the way you want. Much of the art of living is dealing with the unexpected. See with the eyes of a child. Enjoy yourself and celebrate.

C *Cultivate contentment in all circumstances.* Self-doubt is the most daunting of obstacles that inhibit us on our quest for enlightenment. We can know true contentment when we embrace the present and stop struggling to escape insecurity, pain, and doubt.

D *Duality is the central organizing principle of our reality.* We cannot know what light is unless we know darkness. We cannot know the meaning of sweet without knowing the meaning of sour. It follows that we cannot know what we like without also experiencing that which we do not like.

E *Express yourself creatively.* You need to be appreciated for who you really are, so speak and let others know. Communication begins with an effort to make yourself clearly understood. It is easy to let fear and preconceived notions stand in the way of true communication. Also, taking an interest in how others express themselves (known as listening!) leads to sharing, and sharing leads to caring. Creative self-expression is true spirituality.

F *Forgiveness is an antidote to pain.* All too often the tendency is not to try to solve the problem but to fix the blame. It is not a weakness but the greatest strength to forgive. Especially, forgive yourself. Accept your human frailty as a natural part of your being, and your mistakes as signs of your efforts to grow.

G *Growth comes through self-examination and self-awareness.* Know thyself. In our case, it was our commitment to our mutual goal of personal development that has allowed us to learn and help each other grow. We may not know the meaning of life, but we have come to know the meaning of our life.

H *Having a sense of humor is a tremendous asset when it comes to relationships.* It is one of the most valuable and attractive features a person can have. If you can keep looking for the humor in your situation, not only will you find it, it can get you through practically any difficult time. It helps you to keep going forward, even in the face of defeat.

I *Intuition is your inner vision—let it guide you.* Become aware, pay attention, listen—develop a psychic sense of your and your partner's true feelings. Validate each other's intuition. By observing our reactions to the messages offered to us by our intuition, we come to better understand our desires, our goals, and their motivations. We come to see what blocks us, what releases us out of our false selves, and what helps us to meet the challenge of our personal vision and myth.

J *Judgment has its time and place.* Let it help you be relentless in your pursuit of truth and the deeper implications of whatever situation you are in. Remember, criticism must be constructive, not a smokescreen for hurtful words and deeds. Judge the truth and judge the lies.

K *Know that you have the power to defeat negative thinking and behavior.* Learn to understand and cope with your greatest enemy: your own fear. We have learned that living a successful life of quality and meaning does not mean that you won't react to fear, uncertainty, or rejection. What is important is how quickly you recover your equilibrium and get on with the business of living.

L *Love makes a sacred space in our lives where true growth and healing can happen.* When we love and are loved, we have someone we can trust to advise us, someone who has our best interests at heart. When you love someone, you want to be with him or her as much as possible, because committed happiness makes life seem very short, indeed.

M *Make magic, pray, consult the wise.* Real magic is when you concentrate on what you love, not what you hate. Believe that there are unseen forces that protect, connect, and sustain us. When you see the hidden connections, the world becomes charged with symbolic meanings. Magic rituals and prayers help us to remember our connection to these unlimited energies that nurture and beckon us to reach our full potential, and that we will do the work necessary to keep that connection clear and unbroken. Prayer is a form of magic in which we seek to ally ourselves with the Divine.

N *Nature teaches us about the cycles of life.* The entire world is alive with messages, and it speaks to us, if we will only listen. Nature reminds us of the abundant beauty present in everyday life. Make a time and space in your day when and where you won't be disturbed, so you can listen to all that is good in your life "speak." The goal is to be so in harmony with life's purpose that we will instinctively know which paths to follow from the many that present themselves each day.

O *Observe how your habitual thoughts affect your life.* It is the nature of habits to rule us unless we first become aware that they are habits, examine the events that gave rise to them, and become aware of how they actively influence us. The only way to eliminate a habit is through patient awareness and the belief that your life will change for the better if you stop acting or thinking in the old habitual way

P *Peace begins when expectations end.* There is a goodness in things as they are—accept the greater purpose behind frustrating circumstances. The present moment is your point of power. The secret of contentment can't be gained from achievements in the world but only from finding our inner peace.

Q *Quest for truth.* When you have taken the time and done the work of establishing initial truthfulness and trust, you will find that it frees up an incredible amount of energy that can be used to accomplish many important things. Remember, you cannot be truthful with another person unless you are first truthful with yourself.

R *Respect yourself and show that same respect for others.* If you find it difficult to respect yourself, be aware that the most respectable people also have feelings of self-doubt. Self-doubt may never leave, but those who come to respect themselves learn to accept themselves as they are. Root out prejudiced ideas in yourself, and be aware of them in others. Equal partners make successful relationships. There is no other way.

S *Soul Mates work on their relationships by working on themselves.* You know you have found your Soul Mate when you enjoy just watching your partner live, and when you desire to make your partnership work and to be there for each other in every way.

T *Trust the process.* Have faith that there is a divine plan. Worry only creates stress and accomplishes nothing. If you realize that most difficulties you encounter are for the best in the long run, you manifest the positive attitude that can bring wonderful relationships to you. All you have to do is follow your heart, take small steps forward on your path, and trust. Let the future wait and take care of itself. Take time to be in the moment, and experience life with a gentle purity.

U *Unconditional love helps you be more understanding.* Your lover is your best friend—you must be there for each other in every way. You must feel you can trust one another completely and can turn to each other for support and gentle guidance when one of you feels weak. Remember, a maternal nature exists in us all.

V *Visualize your wishes in your mind's eye.* Become aware of the tone and subject matter of your moment-to-moment inner dialogue. Visualize what it is you want with all your heart. See it with your inner sight and feel it as if you were really there, experiencing it with all of your senses. Practice visualization every day. Our dreams help us to create our material reality as surely as our material reality helps us to create our dreams.

W *Working toward goals together is the essence of a living, breathing partnership.* Give support as needed. Concentrate and focus your energy on positive goals: health, fitness, creativity, spiritual growth. When you share love, you can enjoy knowing that you are helping your partner to live to the fullest. This is the secret of true joy and happiness in a committed relationship. Our relationship is as successful as it is because we have both decided it is the most important thing in our lives.

X *XOX—Kisses and Hugs are very important.* Physical touch is the healing catalyst that allows your souls to connect and become one. Sex is one of the highest forms of expression when combined with true love. It is heightened and enlightened by mutual intimacy, trust, and joyful commitment. Without love, sex becomes just another way we avoid feeling empty. Real love is exciting because the two of you care so much about each other and want to show it in every way.

Y *You can only change yourself; you cannot change anyone else.* You can, however, make sure you get involved with a person who desires change for the better. Devoting time to self-improvement or study will always enable you to improve your situation. The desire to grow is one of our most basic needs.

Z *Z-Z-Z—Get enough rest and take care of your stress.* Listen to your dreams. Practice calm. Slow down your breathing. Manage your time. Know your stress triggers. Laugh as much as possible. Get massages. Explore healing practices designed to cure problems on physical, mental, and spiritual levels. You must heal yourself before you can help others to heal.

Also by Amy Zerner and Monte Farber

* Denotes a title that was both created and packaged by Zerner/Farber Editions, Ltd.

* *The Enchanted Astrologer* book and card set, Thomas Dunne Books/St. Martin's Press. ISBN 0-312-25173-4

Gifts of The Goddess: 36 affirmation cards, Chronicle Books. ISBN 0-8118-2729-1

* *The Pathfinder Psychic Talking Board,* Journey Editions/Tuttle Publishing. ISBN 1-885203-89-6

* *The Oracle of the Goddess* book and card set, Thomas Dunne Books/St. Martin's Press. ISBN 0-312-19179-0

* *The Instant Tarot Reader* book and card set, Thomas Dunne Books/St. Martin's Press. ISBN 0-312-16681-6

* *The Zerner/Farber Tarot Deck,* U.S. Games. ISBN 1-57281-073-4

Cupid Cards book and card set, Penguin Books. ISBN 0-67-085747-5

The Enchanted Tarot CD-ROM, Enteractive. ISBN-1-887233-05-9

Paradise Found: The Visionary Art of Amy Zerner (foreword by Rose C. S. Slivka), Journey Editions/Tuttle Publishing. ISBN 1-885203-11-X

The Dream Quilt (children's book by Amy and Jessie Spicer Zerner), Journey Editions/Tuttle Publishing. ISBN 0-8048-1999-8

The Alchemist CD-ROM, Enteractive. ISBN 1-887233-02-4

Scheherazade's Cat (children's book by Amy and Jessie Spicer Zerner), Journey Editions/Tuttle Publishing. ISBN 0-8048-1807-X

* *The Psychic Circle: The Magical Message Board,* Fireside/Simon & Schuster. ISBN 0-671-86645-1

Zen ABC (children's book by Amy and Jessie Spicer Zerner), Journey Editions/Tuttle Publishing. ISBN 0-8048-1806-1

* *Goddess Guide Me: The Oracle That Answers Questions of the Heart,* Fireside/Simon & Schuster. ISBN 0-671-77832-3

* *The Alchemist: The Formula for Turning Your Life to Gold,* Thomas Dunne Books/St. Martin's Press. ISBN 0-312-06181-1

The Enchanted Tarot book and card set, Thomas Dunne Books/St. Martin's Press. ISBN 0-312-05079-8

Karma Cards: A New Age Guide to Your Future Through Astrology, Penguin Books. ISBN 0-14-015487-6

To contact Monte and Amy:
Telephone: 800-308-3578
Website: *www.theenchantedworld.com*
Email: monte4amy@theenchantedworld.com